I0801214

Campus Ministry

Empowering Congregations to Support Students at Colleges and Universities

Colleen Hallagan Preuninger

DISCIPLESHIP RESOURCES

CAMPUS MINISTRY: Empowering Congregations to Support Students at Colleges and Universities
Copyright © 2020 by Colleen Hallagan Preuninger.
All rights reserved.

No part of this book may be reproduced in any manner whatsoever without permission except for brief quotations embodied in critical articles or reviews. For information, write Discipleship Resources®, 1908 Grand Avenue, Nashville, TN 37212.

Discipleship Resources® and design logos are trademarks owned by The Upper Room®, Nashville, Tennessee. All rights reserved.

At the time of publication all website references in this book were valid. However, due to the fluid nature of the Internet some addresses may have changed or the content may no longer be relevant.

All scripture quotations are taken from the New Revised Standard Version Bible, copyright © 1989 National Council of the Churches of Christ in the United States of America. Used by permission. All rights reserved.

Cover design: Ed Maksimowicz
Cover imagery: Depositphotos
Typesetting and interior design: PerfecType | Nashville, TN

ISBNs
978-0-88177-935-6 (print)
978-0-88177-936-3 (mobi)
978-0-88177-937-0 (ePub)

To my beloved students:
Hope and peace and love and trust, all the world is all of us.

CONTENTS

ACKNOWLEDGMENTS

It has been my deep joy to steep in the stories of communities engaged in the work of serving students. In the midst of the turmoil and heartbreak of the journey toward and away from the 2019 special called session of The United Methodist Church's General Conference in St. Louis, Missouri, the stories of congregations and campus ministers contained in this book have been a flame kindled in the dark. Thank you to all who offered your time and energy to share your stories in this resource: Rev. Joey Heath-Mason, Patrick Landau, Rev. Lora Andrews, Rev. Ben Hanne, Megan Otto, Rev. Bill Frisbie, Deaconess Jeanne Roe Smith, Audun Westad, Marianne Munz, Rev. Maria Pedersen-Mong, Rev. Meghan Roth Clayton, Rev. Doug Gestwick, Rev. Steve Darr, Rev. Geoff Helton, and Rev. Carl Chapman. Thank you to the gracious Spiritual Life team at Shenandoah University for allowing space for this project; to my spouse, Rev. Nick Preuninger, and my mother, Lucina Hallagan, for their faithful support; and most of all to my students, who inspire a future filled with hope.

PREFACE

I served as the United Methodist Ecumenical Chaplain at Syracuse University in Syracuse, New York. It was my dream job. This historic chaplaincy, founded in 1871 with the establishment of the university (as a United Methodist school), allowed me to engage in ministry with students at a crucial and formative time in their identity and faith formation. As chaplain, I had access to resources across the university to support my work of serving students with programs and presence in ways that met their needs each semester. Funded primarily though the budget of the Upper New York Annual Conference of The United Methodist Church, I believed I had all I needed to build a nimble and relevant student-centered ministry on campus as a full-time chaplain with a small program budget. As a fully funded campus ministry, our chaplaincy did not depend significantly on outside sources of income or volunteers; denominational funding and access to co-curricular university grants covered our financial needs. We were thriving and excited about ministry on campus, but we were isolated from the work of local congregations.

Despite our long history in the city of Syracuse, the Syracuse chaplaincy did not have many genuine relationships with local congregations. Apart from a few superficial fundraising relationships with congregations in the Syracuse suburbs, the chaplaincy did not effectively partner with laity or clergy from local congregations. There were many nuanced reasons for the disconnect between local congregations and the Syracuse chaplaincy: declining and aging membership in local churches; deep poverty and racial segregation between the city of Syracuse and the relatively affluent, predominantly white surrounding suburbs; a general ambivalence from the chaplaincy staff about investing in the connectional work necessary to build (and rebuild) relationships with local congregations.

In February 2016, the stable circumstances of the Syracuse chaplaincy changed when I was notified by the annual conference of significant funding changes in the chaplain salary and program budget of the Syracuse chaplaincy for the new appointment year. Over the course of a few bleak midwinter weeks, it became clear that the sudden funding changes would require a significant reduction (or possible elimination) of the chaplain position and an elimination of the program budget through the denomination. Suddenly, the once seemingly stable and sustainable model for campus ministry slipped away, leaving the staff and student leaders of our chaplaincy scrambling to assemble a new approach for the fall semester. All at once, the lack of meaningful congregational partners became a cavernous void; the season that followed would have unfolded much differently had the Syracuse chaplaincy maintained and cultivated meaningful and substantive congregational relationships. In a season of plenty, the leadership of the Syracuse chaplaincy did not feel the urgent need to partner with local congregations. In a season of scarcity, ministry with and for students on campus suffered because those relationships were not there.

The fierce and faithful advocacy of laity and clergy on the annual conference floor on behalf of our students in May 2016 restored partial funding for the Syracuse chaplaincy in time for the fall semester, yet much painful discovery was made in the process. As the chaplain who transitioned student leadership through the winter and spring of 2016, making the heartbreaking departure from campus July 1, the deep need for meaningful and stable congregational partnerships remained at the forefront of my consciousness. This project is driven in part by the pain of my own complicity in allowing the Syracuse chaplaincy to operate without meaningful congregational partnerships in a season of financial plenty. Because I, as the chaplain, did not feel the urgency of financial need, I did not intentionally cultivate the kind of congregational partnerships that could support our students with meaningful ministry on campus without a paid staff presence. Although the Syracuse chaplaincy has a happy ending with a part-time chaplain hired to continue the work, the lessons I learned about the sustainability and vulnerability of student ministry inspire me to seek to help others avoid the mistakes made at Syracuse. I believe the answer, in part, is to equip laity in local congregations with concrete tools to discern God's call to serve students on college campuses in their own contexts.

The face of ministry with students on college campuses is always changing; as each semester ebbs and flows, so too do student needs during the rich and formative time of identity and faith formation. Even as mainline Christian churches continue to decline in membership, especially among 18- to 26-year-olds, many congregations struggle to connect in meaningful ways with college and university students in their local contexts. Although there exist examples of thriving ministry with students on college campuses at the congregational level, many congregations do not feel that they have adequate tools to create such ministries. This is the condition that this book, and its companion lay servant course, seeks to address. It is written with the hope that through the process of discernment, goal-setting, and question-asking, this book might help empower the congregational leadership in your church to begin the process of establishing or strengthening ministries with students in your local community.

INTRODUCTION

Toward a Student-Centered Model of Student Ministries

Young people are not the future of the church. They *are* the church, and they are individually members of it. A good student ministry will treat them accordingly. With that said, it is clear that many congregations struggle to integrate young people fully into the life of the church, alienating a younger demographic to the extent that they are all but missing from local congregations across the United States. This, of course, is not true in all circumstances, but it is true in enough communities to raise a significant concern.

It is no secret that The United Methodist Church in North America is in a season of anxiety. Decades of membership decline, aging congregations, denominational infighting, doctrinal disputes, and participation in culture wars have led many Christian denominations to ask serious questions about schism, sustainability, and God's call on the communal life of Christian communities. This has been well noted by scholars and remains an ever-present challenge for the leadership of local congregations across the United States. In the midst of the conversation about denominational decline, many have begun to realize that the American church not only is failing to consistently reach younger people in a way that is relevant to their everyday lives but also is failing to partner effectively with the institutions of higher education where ministries with young people are thriving or have the potential to thrive. Acknowledging this reality in the North American church helps locate God's call for the church to meet the needs of students in the particularity of this historical moment; without acknowledging the anxiety and fear surrounding the current condition of The United Methodist Church, your congregation will be unable to assess honestly the motivation and expectations for starting or strengthening ministry with students. Only with humble self-awareness, intentional discernment, and honest goal setting can a congregation create or support a ministry that is truly student-centered and relevant to evolving student need.

To be in ministry with students, your student ministry must place students at the center and be as adaptive and flexible as college life itself; to meet the real needs of students, those responding to God's call to be in relationship with college students must be aware and responsive to the particularity of their unique context. If God is calling your congregation to this work, God is seeking to place student needs at the center of your ministry. This means that to do this work, your congregation must choose to become intentionally aware of the congregation's own motivations, expectations, and goals in creating a student ministry and must seek out ways to gain student input and feedback as your ministry evolves over time. If your congregation is unwilling to truly place student needs at the center of your student ministry, you should not continue with the process of creating a student ministry. God would not call you to create and build a student ministry that did not specifically serve the needs of the students God is calling you to serve. God is not calling you to create a student ministry to serve your congregation's anxious concern that there are not enough young people in worship on Sunday morning or to ensure that the specific traditions of your congregation live long into the future. God is calling you to serve students, not yourselves. The student ministry God is calling you to create is not about you. It's about the students you serve. This means that congregations seeking to serve students must be aware of their institutional context as well as willing to respond to the changing needs of students within their social, cultural, and institutional contexts, semester to semester and year to year. To engage effectively in this work, congregations must commit to a continual process of awareness and responsiveness to the real and expressed needs of the students they seek to serve.

1

Understanding the Landscape

Locating Your Congregation Within Your Context and Encountering Student Needs

The importance of understanding your context cannot be overstated. Without a clear and intentional commitment to understanding the history, culture, structure, expectations, and assumptions of your congregation and the institution at which your students study, it is unlikely your congregation will be able to create or nurture a vital and relevant student ministry. The way ministry manifests on college and university campuses differs greatly, depending on context. Locating your congregation within the particularity of your context is essential to starting the process of discernment and building a ministry partnership with an institution of higher education.

At some institutions, denominational and ecumenical Christian ministries have been responding to the needs of young people with thoughtful and innovative ministry for decades. Many United Methodist-related institutions have a superb legacy of innovative programming on campus and partnerships with other institutions, equipping students to discern and live out their vocational lives as change agents in the world. These thriving ministries have varying connection to local congregations, and many struggle to connect meaningfully with local faith communities. Some campus ministries, such as the examples highlighted in chapters 2 through 4 of this text, cultivate meaningful partnerships with local congregations. Others, as with my experience while serving as chaplain at Syracuse University, thrive in ministry despite having loose or nonexistent partnerships with the local church. Still others, most notably at state universities or community colleges, have little or no formal ministry organized on campus through the institution. In each of these examples, ministry can be created or enhanced through local congregations if approached in a way that is appropriate and sanctioned by the institution of higher education in question.

As your congregation begins the journey of discernment toward creating or strengthening your ministry with students on a college campus, it is vital for you to understand the landscape of higher education in the United States. Equipped with this information, you will be better able to locate yourself, your congregation, and the institution with which you hope to partner and determine your next faithful step in God's call to serve students. In this chapter, I will outline the general categories of institutions of higher learning, structures of offices of spiritual and religious life, parachurch organizations, and denominational campus ministry organizations that exist today in the United States.

As we begin, it is imperative to emphasize that this information is meant as a starting point, not a comprehensive authority on all models and manifestations of ministry on every campus in the United States. Although it is possible to broadly define and describe the structure of ministry on college campuses by institutional category, there will inevitably be exceptions to the rule. The nuances of campus ministries manifest differently on each college campus. This means that those who wish to reach students by partnering with institutions of higher learning not only must have a general knowledge of the kind of institution with which they are working but also must know the right questions to ask in order to discover the nuanced complexities of relationship building needed to gain appropriate access to students. This chapter seeks to offer you the tools to orient yourself within the particularity of your own institutional landscape, so that you will be able to discern your next best steps in creating or strengthening a student ministry.

Higher Education Categories in the United States

The first step to understanding your context is to locate the institution with which you seek to partner within *its own* context; once you have located yourself and the institution with which you hope to partner, you will be better situated to cultivate the relationships necessary to create or strengthen your ministry with students. While it is not always necessary to partner directly with the college or university where the students you seek to serve are studying, understanding the institutional landscape is an important step in building a sustainable and informed student ministry in your congregation. Generally speaking, institutions of higher education fall into two major categories in the United States: public institutions and private institutions. The difference between these types of schools is the primary source of institutional funding: Public institutions use public funds as the primary source of support, and private institutions are funded primarily through private sources. Each college or university within these broad categories operates with its own particularities, but knowing whether the institution in your context is public or private will help you better craft your approach to potential partnerships to serve in ministry with students who study there.

Public Institutions

Public colleges and universities are institutions funded primarily through the state, often offering significantly lower tuition costs than their private counterparts. Most public universities were originally founded by states and continue to run as state universities. Examples of such institutions include the University of California, Los Angeles; the University of Virginia; and the University of Texas at Austin. Not all public institutions bear the "state university" title, including schools such as the College of William & Mary, the Georgia Institute of Technology, and Columbia University. Each of these schools shares in common a significant subsidy by a state government and a commitment to serve the emerging needs of the communities in which it is located. A range of degrees is offered at public universities, including undergraduate, master's level, and various terminal degrees.

If the institution with which you are seeking to partner is a public university, it is important to understand that the relationship between public universities and organized religions mirrors that of the United States federal government. It is unlikely that there will be any office or official, such as a chaplain or dean, devoted to the care of spiritual or religious life. This means that accessing students for the purpose of ministry, as well as the shape of your congregation-based student ministry, may not involve formal institutional partnership between your congregation and the university. This also means that it may be more difficult to obtain necessary formal permissions to engage in ministry on campus. Many congregations in ministry with students at state universities across the country have responded to this challenge by using church property that is close to campus to create a designated space for their ministry program and support. Student ministries based out of University United Methodist Church in Austin, Texas, are a strong example of this approach, effectively leveraging their physical proximity to public intuitions to create space for student ministries. Other congregations choose to support the Wesley Foundations that serve many public universities as their primary connection with students on campus. Examples of both approaches are outlined in chapter 3 of this book.

Private Institutions

The second major category of higher-education institutions is private colleges and universities. These institutions range greatly in size and affiliation. Many private schools were founded by Christian denominations, though many subsequently have distanced themselves from official affiliation with the Christian tradition. For any particular institution, exploring and doing research using the official college website will be helpful in orienting you to the history and level of denominational or religious affiliation claimed by the institution and also the kinds of services offered for spiritual and religious life on campus. Knowing the history, affiliation, and structure of religious life on campus will be invaluable in creating relationships and gaining the necessary permissions to interact with students on campus.

If you are seeking to partner with a private college or university, it is likely that your congregation will need to cultivate trust-filled relationships within the university's office that is tasked with organizing spiritual and religious life on campus. Sometimes this office is called a chapel (as it is with Hendricks Chapel at Syracuse University), while in other locations it is called an office of religious and/or spiritual life (like the Office of Spiritual Life at Shenandoah University). In other places, the spiritual life of students is cared for through interfaith or multifaith centers (such as the Kay Spiritual Life Center at American University) or by offices with a completely different name (such as the Office of Mission and Ministry at Gonzaga University). In some cases, care for spiritual life is decentralized to particular staff roles without a formal office (such as the "campus ministry" at Southwestern College). As confusing as this can be, in the case of private colleges, it will be important to discover who on campus has the authority to create partnerships with local congregations.

Community Colleges

Community colleges are among the most prevalent and accessible forms of higher education in the United States. The United States Department of Education reports that there are more than 1,400 community colleges in the United States, of which about two-thirds are public and one-third are private.[1] Generally offering two-year associate degrees and a variety of vocational training opportunities, community colleges seek to reach underserved and underrepresented student populations in communities across the country. Often overlooked in the conversation about college ministry, community colleges offer an exciting opportunity for congregations to support nontraditional students already rooted in the local community. I would encourage every congregation that is currently discerning a call to serve students to consider how serving students at the local community college may be a part of that call.

Created as a means to strengthen the local community in which it exists, community colleges are continually looking for community partners with compatible goals; often operating with much less funding than their four-year sibling institutions, community colleges continually seek to expand services and partnerships in the local community as a means to serve the students and strengthen the community as a whole. This outwardly oriented posture toward institutional partnerships, coupled with predominant student demographics of underserved and underrepresented local populations, can make community colleges an ideal location for congregations seeking to respond to a call to student ministry.

Despite the strong overlap between the mission of many community colleges and local congregations, there are not many thriving examples of community college-focused student ministries. While several strong examples of regionally based community college ministries exist (such as the example from Virginia outlined in chapter 4 of this book), this remains a largely untapped opportunity. The reason community colleges are often overlooked in the conversation about college ministry is frequently related to populations they serve; whether we like to admit it or not, too often congregations overlook the unique needs of community college students because those students do not always reflect the needs of younger students studying at four-year undergraduate institutions. Support for community college students may manifest in ways similar to other kinds of ministries in the local congregation: rent and utilities support, childcare, or other essential services. Providing this kind of support is often less desirable for congregations because it does not come with the nostalgic energy of late-night pizza and ice-cream giveaways or the secret hope of welcoming more twenty-something worshipers on Sunday morning. We will address these vices of congregational ego and expectations in chapter 5 of this text, where I propose an honest and soul-searching process of communal discernment for your congregation's call to serve students.

Structures of Spiritual and Religious Life

Offices of Spiritual and Religious Life

Most private colleges and universities have an office dedicated to the religious and spiritual needs of the students who study there. The name, staffing level, and institutional location of this office varies greatly from institution to institution, depending on its history, denominational affiliation, and core values. Examples of office names include the following: Office of Spiritual Life, Office of Religious Life, Office of Spiritual and Religious Life, Office of Mission and Ministry, Chapel, or Interfaith Center. This office, whatever it is called, is usually run by someone with the title "dean" or "director." The difference between these titles is not terribly important and usually has more to do with the culture and history of the institution than the particularity of that person's role. For example, someone runs the Office of Spiritual Life at Shenandoah University with the title "dean" and the Office of Spiritual and Religious Life at Bucknell University is run by someone with the title of "director." In these cases, the "dean" and the "director" have similar levels of authority and responsibility, despite the differences in the name of their title. Sometimes the person who runs the office has the title "chaplain," as is often the case at small liberal arts colleges. If this is the case, the chaplain functions in the same way a dean or director would, caring for the spiritual and religious needs of the full student body, not the specific tradition from which she received her credentials.

Chaplaincies and Ecumenical Christian Ministries

Many college campuses, especially at United Methodist-related schools, have officially recognized United Methodist chaplaincies. Other schools may have ecumenical Protestant chaplaincies supported by one or more compatible Protestant Christian denominations. For example, throughout its history, the Methodist chaplaincy at United Methodist-related Syracuse University has been supported financially by American Baptists, the United Church of Christ, and the Presbyterian Church (USA). In the case of Syracuse University, the ecumenical nature of the United Methodist chaplaincy has been reflected in a series of name changes throughout the years, moving from "Protestant Chaplaincy" to "Interdenominational Protestant Chaplaincy" and eventually to its current name, changed in 2013 to reflect the primary source of funding: "United Methodist Ecumenical Chaplaincy."

In some cases, chaplaincies are created and funded through the university itself. In other cases, such as with American University in Washington, D.C., and Syracuse University in New York, chaplaincies exist in a guest–host relationship with the institution. This means that chaplains are often hired and funded outside denominational sources. For United Methodist chaplaincies, often this means that a chaplain is appointed and paid by the local annual conference and is not an employee of the university where the chaplaincy is located. This creates a unique space for the work of chaplains and chaplaincies on campus, allowing additional freedom for direct congregational partnerships and fundraising, as well as a measure of protection in critiquing university policies and administration. For example, the institutional space offered to a chaplain at a university where she is not an employee may allow her (and the congregations with which she partners) to resource and empower student protesters in a way that may be forbidden to university employees. It may not be necessary for local congregations to understand the intricacies of a chaplaincy's relationship to the institution where it is located, but it may be helpful in order to understand the opportunities that are open to congregations interested in partnering with chaplaincies.

If a United Methodist chaplaincy, umbrella Protestant chaplaincy, or ecumenical chaplaincy exists on campus, it will likely be your first point of contact for institutional partnering. Contacting a chaplain directly as the first point of contact may offer a quicker and more direct way to gain necessary permissions to access communication networks, reserve space, and connect with students on campus.

Wesley Foundations and Fellowships

Wesley Foundations are United Methodist organizations supported by local congregations and independent fundraising. They primarily serve students in non-United Methodist-related institutions of higher education. Sometimes Wesley Foundations exist imbedded within local congregations, and some operate out of their own buildings or rented space in close proximity to the campuses they serve (see the example of the Wesley Foundation serving UCLA in chapter 3). Usually, Wesley Foundations are located at large public universities, such as the University of Arkansas, Virginia Tech, and Arizona State University, but they can also be found at private institutions such as Emory and Duke.

Wesley Foundations and Wesley Fellowships are modeled after the example of John Wesley's original "holiness club" at Oxford University and function similarly to United

Methodist ecumenical chaplaincies by offering various worship, study, service, and fellowship opportunities for students of all Christian backgrounds. Wesley Foundations and Wesley Fellowships usually hire both clergy and lay staff to guide their ministry and are often incorporated as a 501(c)3 and supported by a self-governing board. Because of their history and mission, like United Methodist chaplaincies, if a Wesley Foundation or a Wesley Fellowship exists on a campus in your context, it is an ideal place for your congregation to start building relationships to inform the way you seek to serve students in your context. Wesley Foundations depend heavily on congregational partnerships and are usually enthusiastically open to new partnerships in ministry with local congregations.[2]

Other Denominational Organizations

Although some denominational organizations could be considered parachurch organizations (which we will examine next), there are some that inhabit their own category because of their structure. This is particularly true with Catholic and Orthodox organizations such as Newman Centers. These organizations operate in the same spirit as Wesley Foundations for United Methodists, except their staffing is usually directly connected to the appointment structure of particular monastic orders. For example, Newman Centers are Roman Catholic residence and ministry centers located at non-Catholic colleges and universities. These centers are staffed with both priests and laypeople and provide a variety of religious and social services for Catholic students on the campuses where they are located. Generally speaking, denominational organizations that fall into this category target a specific student demographic for specific theological reasons. In the case of Newman Centers, the organization is primarily concerned with supporting the specific sacramental and spiritual needs of Catholic students through a Catholic theological framework.[3] Although most denominationally based ministries in this category are open to partnering across campus and with congregations in their denomination, their willingness to partner with your congregation will likely be dependent on the perceived denominational compatibility between your congregation and the organization. For example, it is unlikely that a Newman Center would be interested in partnering with your congregation unless it is for a specific ecumenical purpose that meets an expressed goal or value of the organization. This, of course, is dependent on the local leadership of each center or organization.

Parachurch Organizations

There are many freestanding parachurch organizations that organize chapters on and around college campuses across the country. Often, these organizations are nondenominational, and they tend to be theologically and socially conservative. These organizations often have paid staff assigned to each chapter of their organization and have varying statuses at the colleges and universities they seek to serve, depending on university policy. Some colleges and universities formally recognize these organizations and give permission for staff to operate on campus like a campus ministry. Others do not formally recognize the organization or give permission for staff to operate on campus unless the group operates as a student-run organization according to university policy. Although the distinction between these two statuses may not readily be apparent in the way the group operates on campus, the distinction is important to know if you hope to partner with any of these organizations. Following are brief descriptions of several well-known parachurch organizations that operate widely in the United States today.

Cru (Campus Crusade for Christ)

Recently rebranded as "Cru" in an attempt to distance itself from the violent connotation of the crusades, Campus Crusade for Christ was founded in 1951 by a student at Fuller Theological Seminary, Bill Bright, together with his wife, Vonette Zachary Bright, as an evangelical movement targeted at college students at UCLA. Conservative and evangelical in nature, Cru has expanded to include areas outside of college ministry, including international missions. Their ministry focuses primarily on small groups, Bible study, notions of purity and faithfulness, and prayer. Programs also include opportunities for students to engage in retreats, international mission opportunities, and demographically targeted affinity groups. Leadership opportunities for students are consistently offered for undergraduate and graduate students through Cru programming but are sometimes limited by gender identity and sexual orientation. Cru branches usually have a designated staff person, financially supported by their own internal fundraising efforts, and are open to partnering with socially and theologically conservative local Christian congregations.[4]

Intervarsity Christian Fellowship

Intervarsity Christian Fellowship claims roots in a British student movement beginning in 1877 in Cambridge, England, moving to the United States in the 1940s as a conservative evangelical movement focused on student ministry. Today, Intervarsity Christian Fellowship operates branches on more than 600 college campuses in the United States and produces training materials, books, and other resources consistent with their stated theological beliefs and core values through their publishing house. Similar to Cru, each Intervarsity chapter has at least one designated staff person, funded through internal fundraising on the part of the staff person. Leadership opportunities for staff and students are limited to cisgender (identifying as the same gender you were assigned at birth) heterosexual people, and this limitation has been the source of several legal challenges since the year 2000. These lawsuits, brought by more than forty campuses, have resulted in discussions about whether Intervarsity's bylaws violate university antidiscrimination policies at several institutions across the United States. Other universities bringing lawsuits against Intervarsity resolved their concerns out of court and allowed student chapters to remain on campus.[5]

Brothers and Sisters in Christ (BASIC)

Conservative and evangelistic in nature, Brothers and Sisters in Christ (BASIC) was founded in 1978 by a student at SUNY Oswego in Oswego, New York, as a means to reach college students. Based primarily in the northeast United States, BASIC operates in a way similar to Cru and Intervarsity in terms of staffing, fundraising, and theological beliefs. Emphasizing the importance of congregational partnerships, BASIC intentionally seeks theologically compatible conservative evangelical churches with which to partner in ministry to college students.[6]

Fellowship of Christian Athletes (FCA)

Founded in 1954 in Norman, Oklahoma, the Fellowship of Christian Athletes seeks to connect the passion for athletics with conservative evangelical theological beliefs. Offering chapters on college campuses across the country, FCA serves student athletes through camps, Bible studies, and other student support services. Staffed by ministry leaders passionate about engaging in evangelical ministry through the lens of sports, local FCA chapters are organized similarly to those of Cru and Intervarsity, but with a greater emphasis on relationships with coaching staff and faculty in each location. Ministry leaders must agree to the FCA statement of faith, core values, and a sexual purity statement (which excludes the leadership or participation of queer youth or adults).[7]

Young Life

Founded in 1939 in Gainsville, Texas, Young Life extended quickly as an international organization seeking to serve young people in the name of Jesus Christ. Early to adopt a focus on creating a multiethnic ministry focus in the 1950s and a focus on youth with disabilities in the 1980s, Young Life has sought to serve some marginalized populations, though it continues to exclude queer youth and adults in its ministry. Operating camps and programming for youth and young adults, Young life chapters exist in communities across the United States and internationally. Clearly expressing a statement of faith and core beliefs on its website, Young Life aligns similarly with other conservative evangelical parachurch organizations in its theological posture and framework.[8]

Orienting Yourself to the Changing Needs of Students

Working with young people, like working with any demographic, requires cultivating an intentional understanding of their expressed and emerging needs, as well as their primary modes of engagement and communication. It probably does not need to be said that young people are not a monolith, and the particular needs of each individual and community will depend on the circumstances of their context. With that said, being aware of major trends in behavior, engagement, and expressed needs will always aid in creating meaningful and authentic intergenerational relationships. While this section seeks to help orient you to the expressed needs of young people (at least as they are at the time this book was written), more important, it offers tools and resources to access the current data, trends, and *zeitgeist* of student culture and needs in a constantly changing landscape. The purpose of this chapter is not to offer exhaustive research and conclusion, but to help orient you to major themes and point you toward additional credible resources that will aid your further discernment of God's call to serve students. Please refer to the conclusion of this book for a list of recommended further reading on this topic; all of the books listed are well researched and well written, and they should serve as valuable resources to you on your journey.

Generational Labels: Aging Millennials and Welcoming Gen Z

Americans are obsessed with identifying and demarcating society into generations. Identifying people in terms of generations allows some measure of self-understanding and understanding others, categorizing people together according to common experiences or cultural expectations. In some ways, these categories can initially be helpful in building relationships, especially in congregations that may be serving as many as six different generations of people: The Silent Generation (1928–1945), Baby Boomers (1946–1964), Gen X (1965–1979), Millennials (1980–1994), Gen Z (1995–2010), and whatever name might come next (2010–?). Understanding the core experiences, values, and communication methods that shape each generation is helpful for creating meaningful relationships, developing intergenerational competencies, and cultivating thriving intergenerational community.

Unfortunately, generational demarcations often are used as a means to segregate and to "other" people of different ages and experiences; instead of trying to engage differences that manifest generationally, we often choose to use generational differences as a means to devalue the needs of others. This is true of every generation and can be starkly seen in aging congregations across the United States as the younger generations (Gen X, Millennials, Gen Z) are dissociating themselves from mainline Christianity. As younger people become less present and involved in congregational settings, intergenerational relationships become less vibrant, and intergenerational understanding and support decreases significantly. The result in many congregations is the misunderstanding of the needs, motivations, and passions of those in other generations: The older generations misunderstand the younger generations, and the younger generations misunderstand the older generations.

The effect is often a dismissal or devaluing of the other in each case: Young people come to be viewed as lazy, disrespectful, and entitled, and older people become labeled as irrelevant, outdated, and prudish. Of course, these characterizations are not true, at least not completely, and they point to a need for congregations to cultivate intergenerational understandings and relationships within each community. While the need for congregations to develop intergenerational competencies and understandings is necessary for the vitality of any ministry in a congregation, it is absolutely essential to create and build an effective student ministry.

For the last fifteen years, the millennial generation has been the traditionally aged demographic studying in our colleges and universities. Born between 1980 and 1994, millennials have been credited with significant technological and cultural innovation and social engagement, expressing increased values of social justice, ecological sustainability, and gender equality. Millennials have also been accused of an array of social ills by older generations, such as killing the napkin industry and living self-indulgent lifestyles fueled by midafternoon brunch and children's participation trophies. The truth of the matter is that the millennial generation, like all generations that preceded it, integrates the current cultural and societal reality into its identity, values, and behaviors.

The general misunderstanding of the millennial generation in the church is amplified by the reality that many millennials are choosing not to engage with Christian congregations on a large scale. This is true of both millennials who did not grow up connected to a Christian congregation in their formative years and also those who did. Statistical data support this trend, indicating that millennials are less likely to identify as Christian or engage with Christian congregations, and they are overall less religious than previous generations:

> By some key measures, Americans ages 18 to 29 are considerably less religious than older Americans. Fewer young adults belong to any particular faith than older people do today. They also are less likely to be affiliated than their parents' and grandparents' generations were when they were young. Fully one-in-four members of the Millennial generation—so called because they were born after 1980 and began to come of age around the year 2000—are unaffiliated with any particular faith. Indeed, Millennials are significantly more unaffiliated than members of Generation X were at a comparable point in their life cycle (20% in the late 1990s) and twice as unaffiliated as Baby Boomers were as young adults (13% in the late 1970s). Young adults also attend religious services less often than older Americans today. And compared with their elders today, fewer young people say that religion is very important in their lives.[9]

This shift, beginning in the early 2000s, has reshaped the ways congregations experience this generation, and it demonstrates significant areas of difference from other generations of Christian Americans. Understanding the shape of the shift that has occurred over the past twenty years, beginning with the coming of age of the oldest millennial in the early 2000s, will greatly help inform the shape and scope of beginning a new student ministry in your congregation.

The youngest named generation, the oldest of which are now in college, is Generation Z. Resting on the same narrative of disillusionment and detachment from the local church begun with Gen X and millennial Americans, scholarship focused on the emerging needs of the current generation emphasizes the need for authenticity, transparency, social justice engagement, and countercultural expression in Christian communities. Also increasingly important, as it is for the millennial generation, is an understanding of the generation's primary modes of communication and expression through technology. This is an important area of attention for those seeking to create and sustain intergenerational community; you do not need to fully understand and use the most popular social media platforms to reach this generation, but you do need to understand it enough to respect it as a valid form of communication. I've included two helpful resources to orient you to the emerging needs of Gen Z in the "For Further Reading" section of this book, but I recommend simply speaking directly to young people born between the years of 1995 and 2015 for the best way to get to know the people you seek to serve.

Meeting the Needs of the 18- to 26-Year-Old Demographic

The traditional age of undergraduate and graduate students will usually fall between 18- and 26-years-old (18–23 for undergraduate students, 22–26 for graduate students). This is, of course, not always the case, especially if your congregation is working with students on a community college campus or a large state university. While not all students fit into the age range of 18- to 26-years-old, if your congregation seeks to work with college students, it is important that you gain a critical awareness of the unique developmental and faith-formation needs for this age demographic.

Much scholarly work has been produced about the developmental and spiritual formation needs of the 18- to 26-year-old student demographic over the past twenty years. Finding relevant scholarship in this area is somewhat difficult, because it seems as soon as a book on a particular demographic of young people is published, it is already out of date. For this reason, it is important for people called into ministry with youth and young adults to balance the timeless elements of the needs of young people with the particular and emerging needs of each generation. It is impossible to fully understand or know all the nuances of every subset of every generation, but it is possible to be grounded in good scholarship in a way that is flexible enough to integrate changing student needs as they emerge. The remaining portion of this chapter will seek to orient you to the major trends in scholarship around identity and faith formation in this age demographic, as well as offer you resources for further reading.

The current season of scholarship that seeks to identify and assess the needs of the youth and the young began in the early 2000s with books such as Kenda Creasy Dean's *Practicing Passion* (2004) and *Almost Christian* (2010), Jeffery Arnett's *Emerging Adulthood* (2004), and Christian Smith's *Souls in Transition* (2009). These books (and others like them) are all now somewhat dated because of the pace at which student needs emerge and change. Even though this generation of scholarship must be read in light of the generational changes that have occurred in the past fifteen years, they contribute to the foundation of how scholars and church leaders currently approach congregational and campus-based ministry with students. This scholarship helps congregational leaders better understand the state of the mainline Christian church in the United States over the past twenty years and how its current state contributes to the steep decline in youth and young-adult engagement in the local church. It's not always easy to hear, especially for those of older generations steeped in the culture of local congregations, but it is necessary for the stakeholders in local congregations to understand and accept their own history in order to move forward.

In order to understand the needs of young people today, the church needs to be aware of the significant shift in Christian culture and expression within the mainline American church as it relates to young people. Despite the churches' best attempts to create relevant and appealing entertainment programming for youth in the 1990s, the qualitative and quantitative data gathered among the millennial generation (and now among the oldest of Gen Z) indicate that not only are the numbers of active 18- to 35-year-olds decreasing in mainline Christian denominations but also the fruit of the churches' catechetical work with children and youth is not yielding biblically literate and theologically engaged teenagers and young adults. The iconic phrase "moralistic therapeutic deism," coined by Christian Smith and expanded upon by Kenda Creasy Dean in her scholarship, describes the belief structure of many American teenagers beginning in the early 2000s. Creasy Dean argues in her body of work that by the time they complete high school, teenagers raised in mainline Christian churches often have a belief structure that does not resemble historic Christian theology or practice. She argues this is a reflection of movements in the wider American church that devalue robust theological engagement and conflate the national ideology of American exceptionalism with Christian history and theology. To be clear, this phenomenon is not the fault of the young people, many of whom in the millennial generation are now adults. The problem instead resides in the teaching of local congregations, and it can be addressed only by treating the systemic issues of congregational identity and practice rooted in biblical literacy, theological engagement, and communal discernment.

Current scholarship in this area focuses primarily on the unique faith formation needs of young people in light of an increasingly secular American culture. Books such as Andrew Root's *Faith Formation in a Secular Age* (2017) do an excellent job of naming and assessing the state of church and society in the 2010s and offering a hopeful theological path for congregations that are genuinely interested in shifting their own culture to meet the changing needs of the youngest generations (and the world).

Other authors seek to address the emerging (and rapidly changing) needs of the current generation through a reimagining of ancient Christian practices through spiritual disciplines. These thoughtful and creative resources, such as David E. MacDonald's *Benedict on Campus (2018)* and Sarah E. Bollinger and Angela R. Olsen's *The Awakened Life (2019)* are two excellent examples of how congregational and collegiate leaders are seeking to meet the unique needs of the emerging generation within the framework of ancient Christian practice and community building. The current edge of scholarship in this area demonstrates that Christian leaders don't necessarily need something new or fancy in order to meet the needs of the current generation (or any generation) of students, but simply a heart willing to reimagine ancient and timeless practices and traditions, steeped in intentional biblical and theological engagement. As counterintuitive as it may seem, sometimes returning to our roots can offer us new paths forward together in ministry.

A Hierarchy of Needs: Don't Assume Physiological and Safety Needs Are Being Met

Maslow's hierarchy of needs is a psychological theory developed by Abraham Maslow in the 1940s to describe various interconnected levels of support and care needed for human flourishing. Usually illustrated as a pyramid, in its most simple form, this theory suggests that without certain basic needs met, such as shelter, food, and physical safety, human beings are limited in their capacity to engage or grow in other areas of their development, spiritually or emotionally. The basic categories on the pyramid, from bottom to top, are: physiological needs (food, shelter, water, sleep), safety (personal, emotional, financial), love and belonging (friendship, family, intimate relationships), esteem (self-esteem, gaining the esteem of others), self-actualization (integrating experiences, setting and meeting goals), and transcendence (spiritual growth).[10]

Although the illustration of a pyramid may seem to oversimplify the interrelated and interconnected nature of human needs, the basic premise is both logical and compelling: It is difficult to focus on anything else in life if basic physiological needs are not met. If applied to a student demographic, this theory suggests that students who do not consistently have their physiological needs met will struggle both with achieving their educational goals as well as growing in their spiritual practice and belief structure. Although many might assume that college students have their basic physiological needs met, increasingly this is not the case. While it is natural for Christian congregations to seek to engage the spiritual and faith formation of the students in their contexts, it is vital to ensure first that the students' physiological needs are being met. "What good is it, my brothers and sisters, if you say you have faith but do not have works? Can faith save you? If a brother or sister is naked and lacks daily food, and one of you says to them, 'Go in peace; keep warm and eat your fill,' and yet you do not supply their bodily needs, what is the good of that?"[11] Just as the writer of James admonished his hearers to approach ministry holistically, giving careful attention to physiological needs of others, so too must congregations called to serve students ensure first that their students' basic needs are being met.

It is difficult to collect dependable data on the true levels of homelessness and food insecurity among university students in the United States, but it is clear that the percentage of students in these categories is on the rise.[12] Student homelessness manifests in many ways and might not always be readily apparent to the outside world.[13] Students unable to secure affordable housing for the semester may respond by living in their cars and showering at the university gym, sleeping on friends' couches or in common spaces on campus such as the library. As a chaplain, I once knew an international student who would stay up all night studying in the library, which was open to students 24/7, and then come and sleep in the chapel lounge during the day, when he wouldn't be removed by campus safety officials. I am ashamed to say, it took us more than a year to realize that this student wasn't simply living an eccentric study rhythm but was unable to find affordable housing and too ashamed to admit his circumstance. With the right awareness and resources, you can learn to identify and intervene to help students who are struggling to meet their basic needs.

There are many approaches taken by congregations and institutions of higher education to address the rising rate of student homelessness and food insecurity. The staff of chaplaincies, Wesley Foundations, and offices of spiritual life encounter this circumstance with some regularity, often partnering with local congregations to find temporary housing with host families in the local community. This is especially common in times of temporary need, such as over winter or summer break, when campus housing is unavailable and students are unable to travel home. This model is sometimes used to address a need for affordable housing during the semester by connecting students to host families who are able to offer free or highly subsidized housing. Some congregations choose to address food insecurity by offering free meal opportunities based in their church buildings or on campus. Some institutions address this need directly, like Hendricks Chapel at Syracuse University, responding to rising student hunger by creating an independent food pantry where students can access nonperishable foods and personal hygiene products directly through the chapel. Other institutions, such as the University of California, Los Angeles, have sought to partner with local faith communities to meet student needs through the creation of the Economic Crisis Response Team in 2009. This team helps serve as a liaison between the university and faith communities with the capacity to feed and house students with acute need. (A powerful example of a congregation-based ministry that grew out of this partnership, the 580 Café and the Students 4 Students housing shelter, is outlined in chapter 3.)

There is no single model to address student homelessness and hunger, but every effective expression of care and support in this area begins with a congregation's desire to create empathetic and compassionate relationships with the students it seeks to serve. If you are in trusting relationship with students, they will be more willing to share with you their needs (even if they are embarrassed), and you will be motivated in love to meet their needs in a way that promotes health and wholeness. From this position of authentic relationship, your congregation will be better able to care for students in the way they need most. As you consider how your congregation may be called to meet the physiological needs of students, bear in mind that the "free food" you offer at events might be the only meal a student will eat that day. Seek to provide healthy and high-quality food choices and make it easy for students to take leftover food home from events. Listen carefully to dietary needs and seek to meet those needs as best as you are able. Most of all, cultivate relationships of trust by your discretion and empathy, being sure not to embarrass or shame students who disclose that they are in need of assistance.

Intersectionality, Mentoring, and Tools for Vocational Discernment

The term "intersectionality" was used for the first time in 1989 by scholar Kimberlé Crenshaw as a way to describe the critical relationship between multiple aspects of a person's identity and the way those intersected aspects interact with the world. Used specifically to address the inextricable intersection of race and gender as a black woman interacting in a white supremacist society, Crenshaw offered the world a new way of addressing the relationship between identity, power, and privilege as individuals, communities, and institutions. Although Crenshaw's work, along with the subsequent scholarship that built on her work, extends to various disciplines, its impact on womanist and liberationist theologies have helped a portion of the church better understand its own location and complicity in systems of oppression and better embody the gospel imperative to serve those most marginalized in any given context. There are many churches, particularly those that are predominantly white, that have not encountered or embraced an understanding of intersectionality. If you are reading this and realize that this sentiment applies to you, stop reading right now, and go and read the following books: M. Shawn Copeland's *Enfleshing Freedom* (2010), Yvette A. Flunder's *Where the Edge Gathers* (2005), and Patrick B. Reyes *Nobody Cries When We Die* (2016) (or at least buy them online and put them on your reading list). Although your students likely will not be consciously aware of these authors or traditions, as a congregation that seeks to serve young people, especially if your congregation is predominantly white, it is essential to cultivate an awareness of intersectionality and the stories of others so that you can unlock the vast potential your congregation has for intergenerational mentoring.

Understanding the interrelatedness and impact of the intersection of aspects of identity such as race, gender identity, sexual orientation, nationality, and immigration or socioeconomic status will help make your congregation, and each individual member of your congregation, better equipped to become increasingly self-aware and practice empathy in relationship with others. The students studying on campuses in your context come from a variety of backgrounds, with a multiplicity of intersecting identities. They are bright and talented and simultaneously are hungry for meaningful relationships, grounding theology, and mentors whom they can trust. In your congregation, you have a wealth of knowledge and resources as a manifestation of the intergenerational body of Christ; you have the capacity to affirm their gifts, offer careful teaching, and provide stable and trusting relationships to help support and guide students through a formative time in their lives. In order to serve in this way, your congregation's members must be willing to do the work necessary to receive students from different backgrounds and different life experiences, especially those with identities that are marginalized within the current cultural, social, and ecclesial structures in the United States. This is especially true in the wake of the 2019 Special Session of the General Conference of The United Methodist Church.

Unlocking the potential for intergenerational mentoring and vocational discernment with young people in your congregation is possible when your congregation commits to doing the work necessary to shift your culture and increase your awareness about your own identity and the expression of student needs. The Fuller Youth Institute produced a fantastic resource in 2016 called *Growing Young*, which outlines a systematic approach for congregations to both shift their culture and increase their awareness of self and others. While it is not necessary to fully shift congregational culture before embarking on the journey to start or grow a student ministry, it will be helpful and formative to do so during the discernment process. (For those who might be interested in a more comprehensive congregational transformation, the Fuller Youth Institute also offers workshops, training, and coaching for congregations interested in living out the process outlined in their book). The authors of *Growing Young* argue that by intentionally cultivating a congregational community that prioritizes young people, nurtures intergenerational relationships, and intentionally seeks to be good neighbors to those in the local community, a congregation will grow in the vitality of all its members, not just its young people. It turns out that cultivating welcoming, empathetic, self-aware, and trust-filled relationships in community is good for everyone.

So, what are you waiting for? Be the mentor you needed when you were young; be trustworthy and seek to understand the stories of those who are different from you; journey with a young person who is seeking his or her vocational path and, who knows, you might just find *your* way as well.

2

Contextual Models for Effective Student Ministry

Private Colleges and Universities

National United Methodist Church and American University, Washington, D.C.

Institutional Location

The relationship between National United Methodist Church and American University has flourished over the last decade. Metropolitan Memorial Church, established in 1852 by an action of the General Conference and opened in 1869, was created with the unique purpose of serving those vocationally transplanted to the nation's capital for wider civil and governmental service. Throughout the early 2000s, Metropolitan Memorial United Methodist Church merged with three other local congregations: Eldbrook UMC (2005), St. Luke's United Methodist Church (2009), and Wesley United Methodist Church (2013), collectively changing the name to "National United Methodist Church" in 2017 to evoke the original intention of the General Conference for the congregation to serve as a flagship United Methodist church in the capital city of the United States.[1] Originally located on Capitol Hill, in 1932 National UMC moved to its current location immediately adjacent to the campus of American University, with additional campuses located at the former Wesley UMC and St. Luke's locations. Committed to intentional discernment and action, the congregation is both geographically and missionally situated for vibrant and relevant connection to the students studying on American University's campus.

United Methodist-related American University, founded in 1893 by an action of Congress, serves the spiritual and religious needs of its student body primarily through the Kay Spiritual Life Center.[2] The Kay Spiritual Life Center is an interfaith center stewarded by a university chaplain who is employed by the university, and it is home to several chaplaincies and campus ministries led by staff employed by outside sponsoring organizations.

One of the many chaplaincies at the Kay Spiritual Life Center is the United Methodist chaplaincy. Historically, the positions of the university chaplain and the United Methodist chaplain have both been held by United Methodist clergy, but the status of each position is different at the university. The university chaplain is hired and paid through American University, and the United Methodist chaplain is appointed directly by the resident bishop of the Baltimore-Washington Annual Conference and paid directly from the annual conference budget.

In the case of American University, the term "chaplain" can be confusing, as it refers both to the university staff position of university chaplain, as well as the individual spiritual and religious leaders who lead "chaplaincies" through the structure of the Kay Spiritual Life Center. While the university chaplain has a secure status and authority as paid university staff, the chaplains of the various chaplaincies derive their status and authority on campus directly from their official relationship to the Kay Spiritual Life Center.

The relationship between the chaplains and the university is that of guest host and guests; through the Kay Spiritual Life Center, American University welcomes appointed chaplains, campus ministers, and other religious staff on campus with the privileges of space and access, but the university does not directly pay or supervise these religious and spiritual leaders. This creates a unique relationship between campus ministries and the university, as well as an additional layer of nuance when exploring the ways individual congregations may gain access to students at American University. Although both American University and National United Methodist Church are connected to the same denominational body, all permission for ministry with students on the campus of American University ultimately resides with the university chaplain as the official religious and spiritual representative on staff. Through the permissions granted through the office of the university chaplain, the United Methodist chaplaincy (and other chaplaincies at the Kay Spiritual Life Center) has the authority to partner with local congregations to serve students on campus.

History and Evolution of Ministry Partnership

Despite its close geographic location, National UMC has not always had a close and flourishing relationship with the United Methodist chaplaincy at American University (AU). In the early 2000s, a pastoral transition at National UMC led to a renewed energy and desire for National UMC to cultivate a vibrant relationship with AU to serve the students. Originating in intentional conversations between the senior pastor at National UMC and the United Methodist chaplain at AU, a new relationship began to grow and flourish. As the relationship between the congregation at National UMC and the United Methodist chaplaincy at AU grew, the congregation began to respond by creating evolving structures of support for the chaplaincy and its students.

With strong pastoral support, the congregation at National UMC welcomed the first of several seminary interns from neighboring Wesley Theological Seminary as the primary contacts in building and nurturing connections with the AU chaplaincy. In addition to adding paid staff, the congregation also assembled a lay-led campus ministry team to support and guide the emerging ministry. Aided by the leadership of young seminarians and a committed lay campus ministry team over the course of a decade, the congregation at National UMC responded to emerging student needs by designating specific funds in the budget each year for campus ministry. Including student ministries in the annual budget allows National UMC to be intentional about the ways in which it creates, nurtures, and supports ministry with students each year. The National UMC budget designates specific funds sent directly to the United Methodist chaplain for programming costs, funds for creating and maintaining a student space in the building at National UMC, and funds to support service and immersion learning trips and conferences for students. This budget, crafted each year with intentional input from the United Methodist chaplain, the campus ministry team, and seminary interns and other paid staff, seeks to address the expressed and emerging student needs on campus.

In addition to monetary support for programming and trips, National UMC decided to designate a specific location in the church building as a lounge for American University students to use any time the church building is open. Originally allocated as office space for paid staff, the student lounge serves as a communal space for students, stocked with snacks and free Wi-Fi, with the intention of making students feel welcome and at home as a part of the congregation. This space also serves as a satellite location for chaplain office hours and chaplaincy programming, which includes a weekly free meal and Bible study for the students.

Programming support from National UMC evolves each semester through their partnership with the United Methodist chaplaincy. Currently, this means direct financial support for the following areas:

- funding the chaplaincy through the church budget;
- a weekly free (or pay-what-you-can) meal and Bible study held in the church building and facilitated by the United Methodist chaplain; and
- a weekly "Free Food Friday" drop-in ministry located in the church building, a home-cooked meal provided once a month for the fellowship time that follows a weekly Sunday-night worship service for students on campus, and an annual service learning trip.

Specific additional support ministries ebb and flow each year with student needs, including small student gatherings in congregation members' homes for informal events, such as holiday cookie baking, laundry washing, or backyard movie nights. Members of the congregation also make themselves available to meet specific student needs, such as hosting international or other long-distance students over winter or spring break, providing home-cooked meals, and other additional intergenerational support for students as needs emerge.

Institutional Partnerships and Relationship Building

As with any relationship, the ministry partnership growing between National UMC and AU requires intentional communication and collaboration to continue to thrive and meet student needs. This partnership did not appear overnight; rather, it developed over the course of a decade of intentional, student-centered discernment and support for American University students. One important aspect of the relationship between the congregation and the United Methodist chaplaincy is the way the congregational leadership embraces and cultivates a relationship with the United Methodist chaplain. Reverend Joey Heath-Mason, the current chaplain, reflects on the significance and impact of feeling welcomed and embraced by the congregation at National UMC. Reverend Heath-Mason reflects on the power of being included in the life of the congregation: "It's an important thing to be present [in the congregation at National UMC], to have a status. I wear my name tag that says "Reverend" on it—and it's one of their name tags that I wear on Sundays—so I look like a part of the congregation."[3] For Rev. Heath-Mason, the simple acts of producing a staff name tag, answering the invitation from the senior pastor to preach, and intentionally including his input with the campus ministry team and budgeting process cultivates a personal feeling of belonging, partnership, and support for the chaplaincy that he deeply appreciates. The sense of hospitality and belonging extended to Rev. Heath-Mason inspires greater trust and collaboration in ministry between the chaplaincy and the congregation.

The relationship between Rev. Heath-Mason and the congregation at National UMC demonstrates that small acts of hospitality and inclusion can have significant impact on the growth and flourishing of potential partnerships in ministry. Reverend Heath-Mason elaborates:

> For me, [National UMC] offers a needed level of support for the chaplaincy. . . . A solo pastor of a local church has support structure for ministry in place with a committee and lay leadership structure and a network of folks who have been there a long time. One thing I've found in campus ministry is that my board meets once a quarter. They are wonderful folks, and if I need them, I can get in contact with them and they will do their best to support me, but on a day by day or week by week basis—I'm kind of doing this on my own. My student leadership is great, but they are also full-time students, and I can't lean on them the same way I could lean on a lay leader in a local church. So, to have National UMC there as a support is really valuable, and I feel very supported.[4]

This support manifests in several ways, including the personal and professional support of the chaplain, financial support for the chaplaincy, and the ability to network within the congregation for mutually edifying ministries with students, as well as simply being able to borrow resources for worship and events.

For example, the willingness of National UMC to allow the United Methodist chaplain to use the church-owned ten-passenger van makes student service and fellowship excursions possible. In an interview, Rev. Heath-Mason reflected on the impact access to the church van has on his ministry: "National UMC has a church van, and they put me on their church insurance. This is a huge cost-saver for us, but it also makes my life so much easier. I can say to students, 'Hey, meet me in the parking lot at National UMC at 3:00 p.m., and we'll leave from there,' and all I have to do is sign out a key in advance."[5] With access to appropriately insured and safe transportation, Rev. Heath-Mason can better serve and equip students in his ministry in a way that would not be possible without the resource of a borrowed vehicle. Although the AU chaplaincy only uses the van four or five times a year, the willingness of National UMC to give the chaplain access to their van and include the appointed chaplain on the church's insurance policy offers a significant benefit to the chaplaincy.

Partnering Across and Beyond the University

Although virtually all of National UMC's ministry with students takes place through their direct relationship with the United Methodist chaplaincy, the congregation also strategically partners with other departments on the campus of American University to meet greater community needs. One example of such a partnership is the "Campus Kitchen" feeding program, spearheaded by National UMC in relationship with American University's Center for Community Engagement and Service.

The Campus Kitchen program, and the many institutional partnerships that make it possible, began through identifying a significant resource: a commercial-grade industrial kitchen located in the building of St. Luke's United Methodist Church, about a mile away from American University. In a period of discernment during a congregational merger, St. Luke's commercial-grade kitchen inspired justice-minded congregational leaders to reach out to local universities and consider partnering with a national organization called "The Campus Kitchen Project." The Campus Kitchen Project is a national nonprofit organization focused on empowering students to reduce food waste by redistributing food from campus dining halls and grocery stores to those who live in food insecurity.[6] Patrick Landau, director of youth at National UMC, describes the operation of the Campus Kitchen program and its relationship to students outside of the United Methodist chaplaincy:

> We are a part of the national Campus Kitchen program; we are the Washington, D.C., branch of that, and it is one place we've had students not just from American University, but also Georgetown [students], George Washington University [students], and others come through the program. We get about 900 volunteers a year for this program, many of whom are students and would be the only consistent connection our congregation has with students that is completely outside the United Methodist chaplaincy.[7]

At American University, National UMC gained access to student volunteers through the Center for Community Engagement and Service (CCES) and through service fraternities, not through the United Methodist chaplaincy. Although most of the student volunteers are not connected to the university chaplaincy or National UMC directly, they are still actively engaged in the ministry of serving the hungry in the city of Washington, D.C.

The Campus Kitchen program is an example of National UMC's partnering missionally with a department of a university to achieve mutually held values and goals outside the direct realm of overtly Christian ministry. Operating outside the authority and access of the United Methodist chaplaincy, however, means National UMC must operate differently when partnering with CCES for the Campus Kitchen program. The location of this ministry as a partnership with a national nonprofit organization, multiple institutions of higher learning in the city, and other communities of faith requires that National UMC approach institutional bridging differently than it does with ministry activities through the United Methodist chaplaincy. Operating in partnership with the chaplaincy offers institutional access to students and resources in ways that are not always possible when partnering directly with other offices on campus. Congregational leaders at National UMC are intentionally aware of this nuance.

> One of the benefits of working directly with the Methodist chaplaincy is it avoids all the questions of how we get permission to be on campus, how we connect to students, and what is the proper engagement with students. Through the United Methodist chaplaincy, we have a direct institutional channel. Working on the Campus Kitchen program felt much more like what people talk about in missional church classes, where you locate a resource and a need, and then you go out into the community to find partners in that community to meet that need. Through that process, we were able to connect to different parts of the universities we are currently partnered with. Most universities have some sort of service engagement department, and that is where we begin.[8]

Despite a mutually beneficial and growing relationship between National UMC and the UM chaplaincy at AU, the congregational leaders discerned that there are multiple ways God is calling their congregation to serve their surrounding student populations and the students in their local community, as well as to mobilize students to serve others in the wider community through strategic institutional partnerships. This allowed them to continue to cultivate relational ministry with American University students, and even to expand and connect with students at Georgetown and George Washington University.

In addition to the Campus Kitchen ministry, National UMC occasionally partners with American University for events outside their relationship with the United Methodist chaplaincy. Most of these events are intended for community outreach and are initiated by the university as part of larger initiatives to connect with communities that neighbor the campus. Often, these events do not directly target students as a primary demographic. In recent years, such events have included the funding of an annual fall community picnic hosted at National UMC as well as a summer outdoor movie night held on campus. These types of occasional partnerships are made possible by the proximity of National UMC's building to AU's campus, as well as by having church members who serve in influential staff positions at the university. Accessing the resources of location and networking provides an additional layer of legitimacy and interest when partnering with university offices outside the United Methodist chaplaincy.

Grace United Methodist Church and Southwestern College, Winfield, Kansas

Institutional Location

Grace United Methodist Church was planted in 1888 by students and professors from United Methodist-related Southwestern College in Winfield, Kansas. Declaring its mission to be "welcoming all to grow in grace together and share God's love on campus, in our community, and in our world," Grace UMC's history of connection with Southwestern College is woven into the fabric of its congregational identity.[9]

Although connection runs deep at Grace UMC, the effectiveness of its ministry with students has ebbed and flowed throughout the years, depending on the interest and commitment of congregational leadership. The current season of flourishing began in the early 2000s, after congregational leadership identified that a distance had grown between the campus ministry leadership and the leadership at Grace UMC. In response to this growing awareness, the congregation sought to address the growing disconnect between students on campus and the congregation by entering into a process of intentional discernment. Birthed from this process, Grace UMC established a team of members deeply passionate and committed to developing a thriving student ministry based in the congregation. This group of laypeople, called the College Care Team, began much-needed healing and bridging work between the congregation and the college for the purpose of serving the students who study on campus. Then, supported by a strategic pastoral appointment, Grace UMC began to ask and answer difficult questions about congregational motivations and expectations. Grace UMC's campus ministry now continues to thrive because of the discernment work the congregation was willing to do.

Originally founded as Southwest Kansas Conference College in 1889, Southwestern College has deep roots in The United Methodist Church.[10] Students on campus, affectionately called "Moundbuilders" because of an iconic welcome ritual of building a mound of stones in the center of campus at the beginning of each new academic year, access Christian ministries primarily through programming provided by the campus minister, who serves on staff at the college. Although the official campus ministry at Southwestern College has deep Methodist roots and is served by a United Methodist clergyperson, Christian ministry on campus is intentionally ecumenical, as it seeks to serve students in a wide range of Christian traditions. Grace UMC has a strong and defined relationship with campus ministry, choosing both to support the campus minister in his work and to provide supplementary congregation-based programming each semester. Students interested in connecting to Christian programming can also choose to engage with programs offered outside campus ministry, including a discipleship program focused on Christian theology and a worship outreach group focused on building the skills of worship leadership.

Telling the story of the congregation's rich history and connection to the college has become central to the current vitality of Grace UMC's student ministry. The current senior pastor at Grace UMC, Rev. Lora Andrews, emphasizes the importance of storytelling in her work to build and nurture the college ministries:

> Our mission statement has always been serving Christ, campus, community, world. Campus has been a part of our mission statement for a very long time. Whether or not we've lived it out well is another thing, but the church's identity has always been connected to Southwestern College, even when we haven't known how to do it well and even when there were tensions with the campus.[11]

Encountering the story of the congregation's past and present relationship with the college occurs in multiple ways: the inclusion of weekly prayers for students in worship; the reiteration of the mission statement during worship and regular team meetings; annual events offered by the congregation, such as homecoming worship and Welcome Week hospitality; as well as other events held both in the church building and on campus. Telling the story from multiple perspectives and in different ways enables the congregation's history to inspire the church community to live into their mission to serve students in new ways.

Reaching back a century, Rev. Andrews recalls a powerful story that occurred in 1919 after a fire destroyed the original church building. As the story goes, after the fire, the congregation could not afford to rebuild. In response, the then-district superintendent addressed the annual conference to request money to pay for a new sanctuary at Grace UMC. In his speech, the district superintendent argued that because of the connection the congregation had with Southwestern College, the annual conference *could not afford not to fund* the project because of the impact Grace UMC had on the lives of the students it served; because of the congregation's vital connection with students at that time, he argued that the sanctuary at Grace UMC "reached to the ends of the earth." Reverend Andrews understands that telling this story, and others like it, is a powerful tool for empowering the congregation to live into God's call to serve students: "As the current pastor, I'm trying to pull back our history and tell it so the congregation can continue to own their identity and call to serve students."[12]

Effective storytelling has enabled Grace UMC to cultivate a congregational culture that views students, as well as Southwestern College, as assets and gifts. Opportunities to remember the story of connection between the congregation and the college are built into the annual rhythm of community life and influence the culture of the congregation. One such opportunity is the annual homecoming worship service hosted by Grace UMC. Each year for the past 134 years, this service has told the story of the connection between the congregation and the college, serving as an annual reminder for the congregation of the importance of their student ministry. Cultivating a posture of openness toward the college and the students who study there enables new and innovative ministries to grow in the life of both institutions.

In this spirit of acceptance and innovation, beginning in 2017 Grace UMC sought to integrate support for students on campus more fully by challenging all church teams to connect to students in some way. In the year that followed, this initiative manifested in creative and fruitful ways: The trustees partnered with the women's volleyball team to complete a wood floor project in the church building; the finance committee made room in the budget to add a music intern for the fiscal year; the children's team partnered with the theater department to have students come and present Bible stories as part of their Sunday school curriculum; and the mission team added additional student partnerships for the observance of Good Friday. The effect of this initiative was powerful and generative for both students and congregation members, cultivating intergenerational relationships between students and congregation members as well as opening new pathways for future events and partnerships.

Institutional Partnering and Ministering in the Gap

The relationship between Grace UMC and the campus ministry at Southwestern College remains vibrant because of mutual respect and intentional boundaries. Reverend Ben Hanne, a United Methodist clergyperson serving as the campus minister at the college, emphasizes the importance of healthy boundaries and lifts up the importance of student involvement in local congregations. In his work as a campus minister, he describes the relationship between his work and that of local congregations as compatible independent ministry with fruitful intersections:

> How we link as college and church is actually fairly limited; we tend to not have many instances where we have direct pairings where both the church and the college are working together on something, but we have lots of intersection points. This allows us to serve our students from a wide range of denominational backgrounds and needs.[13]

These intersection points include churches such as Grace UMC providing for the needs of specific campus events at the request of the campus minister or other university staff. In addition to the independent programming led for students at Grace UMC, the congregation also responds to the needs of the campus ministry upon request—for example, by providing items such as food for fellowship meals following the weekly Wednesday morning worship service held on campus. The congregation also works closely with the office of student life to meet the expressed needs of the campus by providing watermelon for the annual campus-wide welcome ceremony in the fall and welcome goodie bags for freshmen in the residence hall at the beginning of each academic year.

For Grace UMC, supporting campus ministry means communicating closely with the campus minister and other campus leaders, as well as intentional internal discernment about how God is calling the congregation to minister to students in the places where the current campus ministry does not reach. Reverend Lora Andrews describes this space as "the gap," describing her understanding of the role of student ministry at Grace UMC as supplementary to the primary services offered by and through the campus ministry at the college. This delicate balance of creating transparent communication across clear and mutually maintained boundaries allows both campus ministry and the congregation-based student ministries at Grace UMC to effectively serve students in their own way. Serving on the college care team, Rev. Ben Hanne welcomes the opportunity to offer his advice and guidance around current student needs. In return, by welcoming Rev. Hanne as a member of the college care team, the congregation receives invaluable information and institutional credibility through their relationship with Rev. Hanne. Similar to the experience of Rev. Joey Heath-Mason at National UMC in Washington, D.C., welcoming the campus minister into the life of the congregation in meaningful ways reinforces goodwill and positive relationships between the congregation and the campus ministry. This small act of hospitality and inclusion costs nothing and yields much in social capital and positive relationships between congregation and college.

Student-Centered Ministry in the Gap: Multiple Points of Contact and Support

Rev. Ben Hanne, the current campus minister at Southwestern College, believes that the work of the local church is essential to the spiritual and faith formation of students under his care. Local churches have a vital role to play in the lives of the students at Southwestern College, even those students who are heavily involved in the campus ministry he leads.

> I believe fundamentally that the primary source of a student's faith formation is the local church. I don't see my job as replacing the local church; I think that is a bad model of ministry. I've seen people throughout my time in ministry [who] were so into their campus ministry and had no multigenerational care or connection. The result was that their experience was so severed from the wider body of who the church is, that when they finally graduated and tried to find a church, nothing worked for them anymore. When that happens, it is painful. I want students to participate with us . . . but I also want students to build strong relationships with local churches.[14]

From Rev. Hanne's perspective, the multigenerational connection and exposure available through the local church can serve to build necessary competencies not only to grow in faith during college but also to continue to grow and mature in faith after graduation. "A connection with a local church during college helps students transition from collegiate believer to adult believer; if we expect students to make this transition without a connection to a local church, it is as if we are asking them to shift without a clutch."[15] Reverend Hanne argues that cultivating strong relationships between students and local congregations can be mutually beneficial, offering students support and spiritual formation grounded in intergenerational manifestations of community and offering congregations the opportunity to encounter and receive the passionate energy of the students they serve.

> The relationship between students and local congregations works both ways. If you can get students who are passionate and driven, who bring their ideas and energies to the local church, it provides assistance back to the local church because congregations can see that student energy can be directed in positive ways. This is especially true for a church like Grace UMC, where student energies are received so well, and the student perspectives are respected. This is the model where you see students effectively transition[ing] into adulthood and finding a local church home after college.[16]

Grace UMC serves as a powerful example of a congregation that supports and supplements the programmatic offerings of campus ministry while at the same time welcoming and integrating students into the life of their congregation. Crediting the historical and current mission and culture of the congregation, and the particular gift of Rev. Andrews's vision and leadership, Rev. Hanne lifts up the ability of the congregation at Grace UMC to accept and integrate student energies into community life as a model worthy of emulation.

The willingness and ability of Grace UMC to receive, respond to, and integrate student ideas creates interesting and innovative programming in areas unavailable at the college. One significant way Grace UMC meets student needs is through responding to requests for student-driven projects. As in all congregations, the support of stakeholders within the church's committees and the wider congregation is vital to the success of new and innovative programs at Grace UMC. Often, gatekeepers within congregations determine which new ideas are embraced and which are rejected. For example, the board of trustees at Grace UMC offered support and funding for a student-proposed "hammocking" project in 2017. Located directly next to a popular locally owned coffee shop, a student at Southwestern College identified the proximity of the churchyard to the coffee shop as an appealing location to erect poles to hang hammocks. The poles, the students argued, would create a safe and inviting place for students to bring and hang hammocks during the day to fellowship and study in the front yard of the church. Although many of the members of the trustees expressed that they did not fully understand the concept or appeal, they offered both consent and modest funding to install the poles and agreed to the use of their property to host unrestricted access of their property for students interested in hanging hammocks. The permission and modest funding given by the gatekeepers (in this case, the trustees) empowered students' agency and voice within the congregation, created a space for students by students, and communicated that students are fully welcomed and supported as members of the community.

Other ways Grace UMC operates in "the gap" include the following:

- providing scholarships for students interested in traveling on service learning trips organized through campus ministry;
- offering permission for faculty members and students to use the church building for academic classes or small groups;
- providing affordable housing to students by renting apartments owned by the congregation to students at reasonable rates;
- providing small-group opportunities; and
- providing a number of paid student internships.

As with many other student ministries, Grace UMC also provides a significant amount of "free food" opportunities, including a campus-wide watermelon feed at the opening ceremony on campus each fall, ice cream and pizza during finals week, and other similar free food giveaways each semester. While these are all welcome expressions of hospitality, "free food" is never an end unto itself for Grace UMC, as they continually seek to move past strictly transactional ministries with students and toward increasingly relational connections.

Shifting Congregational Mindset: Students as Neighbors

Grace UMC and Southwestern College have always been neighbors, but only recently has Grace UMC intentionally explored how a "neighborly" identity might influence their posture toward the college and its students. The notion of students as neighbors is an increasingly important part of Grace UMC's student ministries. Referring again to the congregation's history, Rev. Andrews emphasizes that for several years, the congregation claimed the name College Hill Church: "Even though our congregation only had the name for two years, it's important for us to know and claim our identity as a neighborhood church. We were built for this neighborhood, this is our mission, and this is who God has called us to be. It's really cool to be able to pull in this history and inspiration in this time and place."[17] Connected to a larger neighboring initiative within the congregation, reviving a posture of neighborliness toward the campus has inspired new and fruitful partnerships with students and campus offices.

The current neighboring initiative at Grace UMC was birthed out of a series of intentional multiweek small-group meetings within the congregation using principles of asset-based community organizing. The purpose of these groups was for the congregation to explore holistically God's call to be neighbors to all those who exist in and around the geographic location of the church building; the students at Southwestern College are one of many groups whom Grace UMC identified as neighbors in this process of discernment. Because of this, the neighboring work initiated by Grace UMC overlaps significantly with other aspects of its ministry. The effect of this overlap is a complex web of connections between students, college staff and faculty, congregation members, and other stakeholders in the local community. Reverend Andrews believes that the effect of this expansive initiative shapes and guides congregational identity, helping the congregation define and redefine who they understand themselves to be in relationship and partnership with others in their local context.

As a part of their neighboring initiative, Grace UMC began to identify new areas of potential partnership not just between the college and their own congregation, but also between the college and other institutions and organizations within the community. An example of one possible partnership discovered through their process was between the college's Division of Student Life and the local domestic violence center. Reverend Andrews describes the process that led to that discovery:

> As a group, we played a game where we would pull [the names of] two organizations in our community out of a hat and had to try to figure out how we could connect them as neighbors as a gift to one another. As a part of this exercise, we started thinking about more possibilities: What if the Division of Student Life partnered with the domestic violence center to raise awareness for students and other people in the community? This process of identifying assets and possible partnerships has been exciting for our congregation.[18]

The excitement and possibilities emerging from the College Hill Neighboring Initiative have created new pathways for partnership, including a significant influence in the work of the campus ministry office that has focused on similar themes of neighboring and service in a recent academic year.

Cost and Benefit

Surprisingly, given the vibrant student ministry at Grace UMC, the direct cost of student ministry for the congregation is quite low. Reverend Andrews estimates that the direct cost of student ministry programming each year totals less than $750, and that money is primarily used for purchasing food and other hospitality items for events. Grace UMC is able to maintain this low budget by identifying preexisting assets within their congregation (such as offering permission to use space) as well as soliciting donations from congregation members for specific events (such as the meals provided to students as a part of the foster program or candy to stuff welcome mugs). This makes Grace United Methodist Church an accessible model for churches of all sizes, but especially small- and mid-sized congregations that cannot afford large budgets to begin or grow a student ministry in their context.

For Grace UMC, congregational vitality is a byproduct of intentional discernment and a focus on students as neighbors. Although Grace UMC exists as a gift and resource for the students it serves, the discernment required for strengthening its student ministry has had the added benefit of increasing the congregation's own vitality. As Rev. Andrews puts it, "We at Grace UMC have shifted our mindset from just handing out things to students to equipping and sending students into the world. There has been a shift in our congregation to intentionally see students as gifts and not simply people to come fill pews." This shift has had a significantly impact on congregational identity and culture. Reverend Andrews sees the fruit and vitality of this new mindset in many ways, especially in the increasing interest in families willing to serve in the "foster student" program each year. In a congregation averaging 140 or 150 worshipers on Sunday mornings, in 2018 Grace UMC was able to match 75 students with foster families for the 2018–2019 academic year. This tripled the number of matched families from the previous year. Reverend Andrews sees this as evidence of a shift in congregational culture toward a student-centered ministry that unapologetically claims and lives into the congregation's mission to be in ministry with students as neighbors. This ability for the congregation to claim their identity in Christ as a call to be a neighbor has cultivated the vitality of the congregation in recent years. Reverend Andrews reflects on the current state of the congregation:

> We have incredible vitality right now [due to the fact that] we have owned our identity in a way we haven't before because of this calling with the neighborhood, which very much includes our connection to Southwestern College. We're also connected to the public school, hospital, prison, and other organizations in our context, but the primary connection with our identity is as a church that neighbors well. It has helped us understand our calling and focus how we engage in ministry, and do that well.[19]

Confidently rooted in Christ's call to serve others as neighbor, the congregation at Grace UMC feels empowered to set expectations and measures of success that reflect the spirit of abundance and vitality present in their call. In this season of ministry, this means that the congregational leadership is focused primarily on cultivating and counting relational points of connection with students. Grace UMC has released the anxiety that comes from measuring success according to the number of students who attend worship, and they have chosen instead to set goals in terms of relationship and connection. This goal frees the congregation to live into their call to accept students fully and unconditionally as they are. Reflecting on the importance of self-aware and welcoming communities of faith in the lives of students who study on his campus, Rev. Hanne identifies the difficulty of translating student needs into goals and measures of success in the local church: "The emotional development and maturity of students, their sense of agency and consequence, is still in various stages of development for students between the ages [of] 18 to 26. This is part of the reason they are the most difficult demographic to connect into the local church."[20] For this reason and many others, it is clear that Rev. Hanne regards the ministries of Grace UMC as complementary to his own work with students on campus, and he lifts them up as a model from which other congregations might draw inspiration in their own calling to serve students in their contexts.

Audubon Park United Methodist Church and Whitworth University; Gonzaga University, Spokane, Washington

Institutional Location

The back page of the Sunday worship bulletin at Audubon United Methodist Church displays an unmistakable message of welcome in a large, orange font: "No one belongs here more than you." As a new worshiper opens the bulletin for the Order of Worship, she encounters a second message of expansive welcome, one that seeks to express an embracing of all peoples from all walks of life, all life experiences, all orientations, all ages, all stages of life, all socio-economic backgrounds, all points across the political spectrum, and all previous experiences or lack of experience with religion and faith in general. Intended as a message of solidarity, this message seeks to communicate the intention of the Audubon Park UMC congregation to welcome expansively and love extravagantly in the name of Jesus. Founded in 1951 as a new church plant, the congregation at Audubon Park UMC began their life together worshiping in a local elementary school as they discerned God's call to serve the city of Spokane. Rooted in a self-identified "progressive evangelical" theology, over the past sixty years the congregation has established itself within the Audubon neighborhood as a vital and expanding ministry, coming full circle in 2018 as a mother church birthing its own church plant called "the Creators' Table" in another Spokane neighborhood.[21] Committed to an intergenerational expression of community life, Audubon Park UMC is in the process of building a student ministry, seeking to authentically reach the college-age demographic noticeably missing from many mainline protestant churches in Spokane. Without any United Methodist-affiliated or UM-related schools in the city, Audubon UMC has begun the process of serving students and creating institutional relationships that exist outside preexisting denominational networks.

Spokane, Washington, is home to two private universities: Whitworth and Gonzaga. Whitworth University, founded in 1890, is a private liberal arts university affiliated with the Presbyterian Church (USA).[22] Gonzaga University, founded in 1887, is a private Catholic university that defines its theological values as "Jesuit, Catholic, and humanistic."[23] Both universities, intentionally affiliated with different Christian traditions, have offices dedicated to the spiritual formation of students but without a specific United Methodist presence or focus. Located in different parts of the city, the campuses of Whitworth and Gonzaga are both between twenty- to twenty-five-minutes' driving distance away from the Audubon Park UMC building. Despite the distance, Audubon Park UMC is in the process of building (and rebuilding) a student-centered ministry based within the congregation to serve the students who study on these campuses.

Institutional Relationships: Do We Always Need Institutional Permission?

The organic and emerging student ministries present at Audubon Park serve students at a variety of institutions: Whitworth University, Gonzaga University, and a variety of local community colleges in Spokane. Created and sustained by leveraging relational networks, the student ministry at Audubon Park depends more on personal relationships than institutional connections. This allows the church to choose whether, and how, to seek formal partnership with the institutions where its students study.

The relationship between Audubon Park and Whitworth is by far the strongest and most mutually beneficial institutional relationship the church has with an institution of higher education. Deepened by the fact that their senior pastor is both a Whitworth graduate and adjunct professor, the congregation has a formal relationship with the institution. Audubon Park UMC is recognized by the university's Office of Spiritual Life, is an approved site for students to complete service hours required through the Office of Service Learning, and offers continuing education classes accessed by members of the congregation. Audubon Park UMC has a positive and mutually edifying intuitional relationship between the congregation and the university.

In contrast to Whitworth University, the institutional relationship between the congregation and Gonzaga University is all but nonexistent. Inspired to initiate an institutional relationship because of an increase in United Methodist students in the 2018 freshman undergraduate class, the congregation's first attempts to build a relationship with the Office of Mission and Ministry at Gonzaga were not successful. With no student leader on campus and no formal institutional connection or permission to operate on campus, Audubon Park UMC began to ask whether a student ministry focused at Gonzaga was even possible and to what extent they needed permission from the university to proceed.

Surprisingly, the congregation discovered that although positive relationships and institutional permission at Gonzaga would be ideal, these are not required to do the work the congregation feels called to do. Reverend Geoff Helton reflects on the church's emerging call and relationship with Gonzaga: "It would make things easier to be officially recognized in terms of reserving space on campus or having better access to communication networks on campus about events, but we can still do what we need to do without all that. It would make our work easier, but it's not necessary."[24] Even though the relationship is not necessary to complete the work, the leaders at Audubon Park UMC continue to find and cultivate new relationships on campus by identifying university staff and faculty already present in their networks. "We're working some other networks to create relationships," Rev. Helton says. "What I've learned is that institutions grow and change as staff turns over." Focused on creating relationships filled with love that serve students, Audubon Park UMC plans to continue to discern the shape of its congregation's ministry with Gonzaga students and how that ministry relates to students at other institutions in Spokane and to their larger ministry to and with young people.

Building Ministry Capacity Through Building Relationships

The current season of student ministry at Audubon United Methodist Church began with a pastoral change in 2013, as the newly appointed senior pastor, Rev. Geoffrey Helton, began the process of relationship building with high school and college students in the Spokane area. The process of building a student ministry at Audubon depends heavily on creating and leveraging relational networks as a resource; located outside of a convenient travel distance from university campuses, congregational leadership at Audubon UMC must rely on the power of relationships to build and grow their student ministry.

Relationship building with students at Audubon UMC takes many forms, beginning with the pastor. Desiring to better know and understand the community the congregation seeks to serve, Rev. Helton began the process of creating and nurturing institutional and personal relationships within his preexisting network. As an alumnus of Whitworth University, reconnecting to faculty, staff, and students on campus was a natural place to start. Reverend Helton began this process by visiting campus regularly, making relationships with the staff in the Office of Spiritual Life and eventually becoming an adjunct professor teaching undergraduate courses. These new relationships allowed Rev. Helton—and, by extension, the congregation at Audubon Park UMC—to establish the congregation as a safe and institutionally trusted place for Whitworth students to connect with an intergenerational congregation. Reverend Helton took a similar approach to connect with high school students by connecting to local United Methodist camp and retreat centers, volunteering one week each summer to serve as the camp pastor. Serving in this way allows Rev. Helton to build authentic relationships with high school students, college-aged seasonal staff, and other similarly committed adults in leadership across the annual conference and in other denominational systems. These relationships help to inform Rev. Helton's understanding of emerging student needs and serve to connect him to an increasing number of young people at critical junctures in their identity and faith formation. Leveraging and nurturing these relational networks has grown the number of students connected to Audubon Park UMC and has guided the church's ministry with those students over time.

The Ebb and Flow of Student Ministry: Student-Focused and Willing to Fail

The approach of outwardly focused relationship building with students at Audubon Park UMC is matched by the cultivation of an inward culture of radical acceptance and flexibility within the congregation. When the congregation began the process of starting ministries to support students in 2013, their first step was to discuss their goals for starting a student ministry with the congregation's stakeholders.

> We began by planting the seeds of conversation in existing small groups about the possibility of starting some sort of student ministry. Eventually, the conversation made it to a committee meeting, and there we talked about how we would want a congregation to respond if one of our students went to college somewhere else and ended up there. We decided we wouldn't want another congregation to use our students. We would want that congregation to love our kids and want what's best for them and to support them. So, in light of that conversation, we decided to build a program around supporting students and helping them grow.[25]

The process of identifying values, expectations, and goals during the first stages of the process allowed the congregation at Audubon Park UMC to establish a student-centered posture at the very beginning of their ministry.

The first concrete step the congregation made to support students was creating employment opportunities for students in the form of paid internships. These internships are funded through the operating budget of the church at a rate of $1,000 per semester. The hope was that by creating paid student-centered internships, the congregation could support students in multiple ways: financially through a stipend, emotionally and spiritually through formative experiences and mentoring, and by providing an opportunity for the students to experience intergenerational community and support during their university years. The student internships themselves are unique, as they are tailored to the specific interests, passions, and vocational aspirations of each student who applies; placing student learning and formation as the goal of each internship, the congregation understands these yearly positions as a way for the church to invest in students' lives at a critical juncture in their personal and professional education and formation.

The internship program that has emerged over the past five years is radically student-centered, often placing student needs above that of the congregation. Instead of the congregation discerning and determining what positions it needs filled by student interns, it asks student interns to discern and determine the scope of their own internship position based on their own needs and sense of call. This posture toward the student interns is foundational for the goals of the program:

> For all of our interns, we are clear with the congregation that the purpose of having student interns is about student learning, not about the church getting work done. Most churches think about internships as a cheap way of filling a position or of starting a ministry, or doing something new. From the beginning of our intern program, we were very clear that we were going to build these positions around what each student wanted.[26]

Over the past five years, Audubon has hired seven different students with internships focusing on areas such as pastoral care, youth ministry, campus ministry, and worship leadership. In each case, the area and focus of the internship was crafted by the student in conversation with pastoral staff and supported through consistent pastoral supervision and mentoring.

Despite the radically student-centered approach to the internship program at Audubon Park UMC, student interns are not always successful in the positions they create; the stresses of college life, the realities of overcommitment, burnout, and the overall transient nature of university life all have the potential to contribute to mediocre engagement on the part of the student. Rejecting a consumerist congregational mindset, Rev. Helton addresses this possibility by intentionally communicating the goal of this ministry to the congregation: We are here to sow extravagant love into the lives of students without the expectation of getting anything in return.

The importance of this posture was particularly evident when one student intern was not able to meet the commitments of the internship, which was focused on building a college ministry on the campus of Gonzaga University. Hiring a student intern passionate in this area was exciting, because Audubon Park UMC did not yet have a campus ministry specifically focused on Gonzaga University. If this student were successful in beginning something at Gonzaga, it might open doors to gaining increased access and building institutional relationships with the university. At the beginning of the semester, there was much potential in the project, but there was also significant risk of congregational disappointment if the project failed. When asked how the congregation prepared itself to set realistic, healthy goals and expectations for this project, Rev. Helton highlighted the importance of honesty and communication: "We were clear in communicating with the congregation that [the lives of] college students are very transient, and college ministries ebb and flow. A congregation might have a strong college ministry program for a few years and then you don't, and that's natural." In the case of the college ministry student intern, due to extenuating circumstances (and an opportunity to study abroad in the spring semester), the creation of a college ministry at Gonzaga did not develop as either the student or the congregation had hoped. Although the student intern created a handful of relationships with Gonzaga University students during the semester, the student was unable to devote the time or energy necessary to fulfill the commitment as a student intern. As the semester progressed, it became clear that the student intern had taken on too many obligations to be successful in both schoolwork and the internship. Nonetheless, the congregation chose to communicate transparently with the student and continued to pay the student's stipend through the end of the semester:

> We are very clear with students that school comes first, so, if something has to give, it's the internship [rather than] school. So, in the [event] that a student who is working for us gets overwhelmed and their grades start to slip, we always decide to fulfill the commitment we make to student interns to pay the student through the end of the semester, but [we] ask them to focus on school.[27]

This expression of honest communication and grace extended by the congregation demonstrates the values established at the creation of the student intern program; although the student was unable to fulfill her commitment, the congregation was able to value her health and formation above work output.

Creating a congregational culture that values student formation over congregational return requires intentional awareness and goal setting on the part of the congregation. It is only in this sort of a setting that a congregation will be willing to consider a student's failure as an important formative experience. At Audubon Park UMC, the church leadership has sought to shape this kind of congregational culture across all ministry areas by framing ministry with the concept of *extravagant love*: "Often, churches put a lot of energy into a program—it could be student ministry or another kind of outreach ministry—and they get resentful when there is not some sort of payback. We have worked really hard to talk about the fact that our job is to love without regard to being paid back."[28] To support this emerging commitment to loving others in this way, the congregation has used Jesus' parable of the sower, inspired by the image of God as an eccentric farmer who sows seed indiscriminately, throwing seed wherever it falls, seemingly unconcerned about the harvest. "This story and image of God has become a powerful narrative for our congregation and for all of our programming. We just love and invest in people, and we don't care whether we get return."[29] Pairing intentional communal study of scripture with other resources such as *Growing Young: Six Essential Strategies to Help Young People Discover and Love Your Church,* by Kara Powell, Jake Mulder, and Brad Griffin (Baker Books, 2016) and resources written by Brené Brown, the congregation has been able to embrace a spirit of vulnerability and self-awareness as they begin to name and acknowledge latent fears. "When we expose our vulnerabilities and fears, they do not rule us in the same way. This work has helped our congregation be less tied to institutional survival and be more authentic to who we are called to be [as] a church."[30]

Setting realistic and student-centered measures of congregational expectations of the emerging student ministries at Audubon Park UMC is essential for the health and sustainability of this congregation-based ministry. Shifting the definition of *success* to focus on the ways the congregation is able to invest in the lives of students allows the program to focus on student impact, not congregational return. "A lot of our work has been around giving up control. Often churches want to dictate what the relationship will be with a student or what a college ministry looks like. Our congregation has decided we don't care about dictating the relationship, we just want to be in relationship because we think we are better when we are in relationship with others." Placing authentic relationships at the center of their definition of success allows the congregation to measure and track data on their student ministries in new ways. Becoming increasingly detached from numbers as a measure of success, the congregation has moved toward a more narrative-focused approach to assessment. In this way, the leadership at Audubon Park United Methodist Church hopes to further influence the culture of the congregation. "Ultimately, you become what you measure. If you are all about numbers, then you become focused on numbers, and the people involved don't matter as much. Whereas, if we can measure stories, then people's stories matter and you can have a deeper relationship with the people you serve."[31]

3

Contextual Models for Effective Student Ministry

Public Universities

University United Methodist Church and University of Texas, Austin, Texas

Institutional Location

The history of University United Methodist Church (UUMC) began in 1887, when Rev. J. E. Stovall started holding worship services in a small building owned by the Northern Methodist Church, located on the then three-year-old University of Texas campus. Over the years, the location of the growing congregation moved several times, eventually settling in its current location on the corner of 24th and Guadalupe streets, directly across from the University of Texas at Austin campus. Honoring the historical connection between the congregation and the university, UUMC continues to find creative and mutually edifying ways to serve the students studying across the street.

The location and history of UUMC serves as a powerful starting point in the congregation's discernment of God's call to serve the students of the University of Texas at Austin. Located directly across from campus, the church building itself provides an excellent opportunity to access students. Megan Otto, the current campus minister on staff at UUMC, reflects on the importance of their church location: "We have the unique position of being directly across the street from the student union, sharing a block with a building that is on campus, which is a close geographic location to campus. We have thousands of students [who] walk by our building every day, which is an amazing opportunity for us."[1] Megan believes that the location of the church building provides an imperative for the congregation to serve the university as their most immediate neighbors:

> We sometimes forget, and I try to continue to remind the congregation, that we do not have a neighborhood around our church: The university *is* the neighborhood around our church. For several blocks in any direction from our church building, it is the university or downtown. This means the people living around us are mostly college students and businesses located around the university, so our mission field is the college students.[2]

Framing ministry with students as the fulfillment of the greatest commandment, the congregation of UUMC seeks both to meet students where they are on campus and to welcome them on their property and in their church building.

The relationship between University United Methodist Church and the United Methodist student ministry at the University of Texas at Austin is particularly interesting because its connection with students on campus currently exists independently from the Wesley Foundation that operates in the same community. Beginning in the 1950s, the Wesley Foundation in Austin has had close connections with UUMC, who initially provided them office and programming space. Throughout the years, the relationship between UUMC and the Wesley Foundation has ebbed and flowed as the two communities have navigated increasing theological differences.

The relationship between the congregation and the Wesley Foundation changed significantly with the Wesley Foundation's purchase of their own building in a different part of the neighborhood. Although both entities operate under the same denominational brand, with the Wesley Foundation's move in the late 1990s, the congregational leadership of University United Methodist Church felt called to create a distinct campus ministry based in their local congregation. Embracing their history as a progressive congregation, UUMC chose to focus on nurturing an intentionally progressive student ministry.

Even so, the congregation continues to seek meaningful and mutually edifying relationships with the leadership of the Wesley Foundation, occasionally partnering for joint projects or programs such as mission trips or service opportunities. Responding to what they discerned as God's call to serve and engage in ministry with students in a new way, in 2002 the congregational leadership at University United Methodist Church began a process of discernment around creating and nurturing an overtly progressive ministry at the University of Texas at Austin.

Programming for and with Students

The types of programming offered for students through University United Methodist Church include a free dinner and worship in the church building every Sunday; a free home-cooked lunch every Wednesday prepared by the UUMC campus ministry staff; and seasonal retreats, excursions, and educational opportunities. Most student programming at UUMC is coordinated through the campus ministry staff person and depends on congregational volunteers who create relationships with the students who participate each week. As with other student ministries, these events often involve free food as a way to meet the students' physical and financial needs. In most cases, the free food is not an end unto itself but rather serves to create an environment where students and congregational leadership can interact and build relationships of trust and support.

While free food is a stereotypical draw for college students, it is important to note that with the rising cost of tuition and living expenses, students are experiencing increasing food security issues at colleges and universities across the country. Free nutritious meals offered as, or alongside, programming often meet a real and pressing need for the students who participate.

In addition to the weekly and seasonal programming offered to students through UUMC, the congregation also offers life-skills workshops, covering topics such as meal preparation, mental health, and sexual education. Unlike traditional educational programming offered by churches, such as Bible studies or book studies, these workshops offer critical information and skills for students living away from home for the first time. Megan Otto, the campus ministry staff person at UUMC, reflects on the purpose and power of these workshops: "I do meal preparation workshops because it is a skill that many students need but do not have. It is expensive to eat out all the time, especially in Austin, and I've found it's very helpful for students to have the skills and confidence to prepare their own meals."[3]

While cooking workshops can help promote a healthy and financially sustainable lifestyle on a student budget, sexual education and mental-health workshops offer equally vital and potentially lifesaving skills and competencies. The purpose of offering sex education workshops within a faith-based context is to equip students with essential knowledge that promotes safe and healthy sexuality during their college years. Megan Otto elaborates:

> [This program is] for students, especially in Texas, [who] may have never had sexual education in their public high school and [have] no information from their parents . . . to have an opportunity to learn what they need to know so they can make the best decisions possible for the health of their own bodies. This program is not purity culture; this is not shaming; this is a program to help students make healthy decisions about their own bodies.[4]

Offered yearly as four- or six-week sessions, UUMC's sexual education workshops seek to meet a real and pressing need for education and provide a safe space for students of faith to engage with information that is often considered to be taboo within the church. As the campus minister, Megan has noticed that the primary demographic who attend these workshops are freshman and sophomore women, a demographic especially vulnerable without access to trusted and comprehensive information about sexual health.

Similar to the sexual education workshops, workshops on mental health and anxiety equip students with essential information and build trusting relationships within the congregation to support and nurture students during difficult times. Responding to a significant increase in self-disclosed depression and anxiety over the last several years, UUMC participated in the pilot program of a new curriculum produced by the General Board of Higher Education and Ministry (GBHEM) titled *The Awakened Life*, which seeks to help students cope with depression and anxiety through spiritual disciplines.[5] Focused on building healthy coping skills, these workshops based on the GBHEM curriculum seek to offer students concrete resources to help them advocate for themselves during difficult times.

Establishing Positive Relationships with a State University

The University of Texas at Austin, like many public institutions, has strict guidelines about how religious organizations can engage with students on campus. Because of this, University United Methodist Church struggles at times to maintain a strong and trusting relationship with university leadership. As a local congregation, it is often difficult to build a direct relationship with a public institution; therefore, congregations like UUMC must carefully explore creative ways to build trust with the institution to gain privileges and access to the campus.

One way University United Methodist Church gains access to the campus is by organizing students involved in their campus ministry to become an officially registered religious organization on campus. By doing this, student leaders become the official liaison to the university, allowing access to promote events on campus, though reserving space or hosting events on campus can still be difficult, even with a recognized student group. Another way UUMC gains access to the campus is by the campus minister's participation in the university interfaith council. This council is composed of campus ministers from throughout the city of Austin, and it seeks to build formal relationships with the university. Through participation in this council, UUMC hopes to build trust and credibility with leaders at the university and better serve the students who study there. Although UUMC is not required to cultivate a relationship with leaders at the university to engage in ministry with students, the church remains committed to doing so in whatever ways it can. Cultivating such relationships through hosting a recognized student religious organization and engaging in the advocacy work of the university interfaith council allow the congregation to better understand the emerging needs of students on campus and seek to meet those needs through its ministry.

Building and Rebuilding: Embracing the Wisdom Offered in Fallow Times

Like many congregations with the name *University United Methodist Church* in college towns across the country, the proximity of the church building to campus heightens disappointments when the congregation is not able to connect effectively with the students it seeks to serve. Despite a long history of supporting a congregation-based campus ministry at UUMC, when a longstanding campus minister retired in 2000, the position remained vacant for two full years until Rev. Bill Frisbie was appointed to the position in January 2002. During the five semesters the campus ministry staff position remained unfilled, the effectiveness of the ministry atrophied. When Rev. Frisbie began the job, there were very few students actively engaged at UUMC, and very few congregation members were engaged in student ministry.

That fallow period between 2000 and 2002 at UUMC offered a unique opportunity for the congregation to gain insight and set new intentions for ministry going forward. As simple as it sounds, one of the insights gained from this period was the importance of designating a leader for the campus ministry. When UUMC's paid staff position was left vacant, it resulted in a significant decrease in the congregation's engagement with students. Reverend Frisbie attributes the withering of the campus ministry program between 2000 and 2002 to the absence of intentional leadership:

> I think there is an erroneous belief that young adults are just going to somehow arrive and organize organically in a congregation. In other words: Congregations need to have a staff person if [they] want a campus ministry. You are not going to have a thriving youth ministry without a youth director or a children's ministry without a children's director, so why should we think that we can have a thriving campus ministry without someone to organize it? That person does not have to be ordained or even full-time, but you have to have a person around whom the ministry can coalesce. Case in point is University United Methodist. In 2002, they were surrounded by 50,000 students studying at the university but had virtually no students attending for several years, in my opinion, because there was no staff person.[6]

Although leadership of student ministry takes many forms in congregational settings, the funding of a paid campus minister position on staff at the church proved to be the most successful approach for UUMC. Once filled, the position offered the opportunity to build relationships with students, cultivate intergenerational relationships within the congregation, and work with students to create relevant and accessible programming.

The foundation for the current student ministry at UUMC under Megan Otto's leadership was created in the early years of Rev. Frisbie's tenure. Beginning with only six students in January 2002, Rev. Frisbie approached the campus ministry as a new program instead of a continuation of a preexisting ministry.

> When I arrived, I sat down with our six students the first night, and I asked for help. It's challenging but also exciting to arrive with a blank page to create and to start over. At that meeting, I asked who among them would be the founding mothers and fathers of the campus ministry in the new millennium. I gave the students a lot of ownership and autonomy in that first semester.[7]

Reverend Frisbie empowered the small group of students to be the founding members of something new. This approach centered around the students' experiences and gave them the agency to envision a ministry that was not tethered to the history or format of what came before. This freedom allowed for the formation of a campus ministry that could meet emerging student needs in ways that may have been impossible before the fallow season.

Motivations for Ministry and Measures of Success

Through the leadership of campus ministers and congregational volunteers, UUMC has slowly rebuilt a sustainable and thriving progressive student ministry over the past two decades. This process of building a sustainable relationship with students requires an intentional awareness of the congregation's expectations and goals for student ministry. If the motivation is simply to have students assimilate into the existing structures by attending worship and showing up for longstanding church events or to have the students serve as cheap labor for the congregation's ministry, the student ministry will not be relevant to the young people it seeks to serve. UUMC's current campus minister, Megan Otto, speaks passionately about the ways churches fail to truly serve students because of a narrow understanding of student ministries:

> What I've found is that we have to change the conversation around why we are doing this. This is a problem that churches located near universities experience all over the country; it's a story I have to advocate for in my work as a campus minister. Students are not an accessory, they aren't your work team, they are not your muscle, and if congregations continue to only view students in this way, they will miss out on all of the opportunities offered to the congregation when they are in ministry with students.[8]

She goes on to argue that many of the churches that try and fail to create effective student ministries do so because their goals and measures of success are misplaced: "Many churches, although they don't mean to, are using the students for their own gains. This is not what we are here to do. We must fundamentally change the conversation and have congregations ask themselves honestly why they feel called to do this work."[9] Megan argues that a significant part of changing the conversation about student ministry is shifting both the motivation and posture of congregations toward students. This includes a radical willingness not only to welcome students into the congregation but also to shift programming, worship, and other aspects of congregational life in response to student needs.

The question of the measure of success is often complicated for congregation-based campus ministries because of the difference between the rhythms of campus and congregational life.

While it is widely accepted that it takes at least three to five years to build an effective campus ministry, congregational leadership often wants to measure success on a shorter timeline. The disconnect between congregational expectations and the realities of campus ministry often produces conflict and unhealthy measures of success. To address this, Megan Otto advocates for open and honest communication within the congregation about the motivations for engaging in student ministry. This kind of open and honest conversation between designated campus ministry leaders and the larger congregation can sometimes be difficult, especially when all parties seek to be faithful stewards of both the call to serve students and the financial resources it takes to support such a ministry. Megan believes that in order to be truly successful in developing a vibrant and relevant student ministry, congregations need to be willing to practice patience and let the fruit grow:

> I think many congregations do not give student ministry programs enough time to grow. Campus ministers end up having to fight tooth and nail to claim the time we need to build our ministry. I think often folks in congregations decide to do campus ministry and after one year only have five students and are tempted to give up. This work is slow work, and to be successful you need to have a church council or lay staff that understands that and supports that work.[10]

580 Café (Wesley Foundation)—University of California, Los Angeles, California

Institutional Location

Located at St. Alban's Episcopal Church, the 580 Café exists as a freestanding Wesley Foundation serving students at the University of California, Los Angeles (UCLA). UCLA is a public university located in Los Angeles, California, with a student body of 35,000. The Wesley Foundation Serving UCLA, known to most in their context as the 580 Café, has gone through significant changes in funding sources in the past decade as part of the larger trend of decreased funding and the decentralization of campus ministries from annual conferences. As a part of this decentralization, the Wesley Foundation receives funding from grants from the California-Pacific Annual Conference of The United Methodist Church, and the executive director of the Wesley Foundation is no longer an employee of the annual conference. This shift officially nests the Wesley Foundation's work within the context of a local congregation. Under the leadership of its executive director and board, the Wesley Foundation remains an independent organization responsible for its own organization, funding, and programming. The Wesley Foundation exists at a unique institutional intersection: a freestanding and self-funded organization incorporated as an independent 501(c)(3), physically located in the building of St. Alban's Episcopal Church and organized as part of Westwood United Methodist Church in the city of Los Angeles.

Deaconess Jeanne Roe Smith currently serves as the executive director of the Wesley Foundation Serving UCLA, a position she has held since January 2009. For Jeanne, her identity as a deaconess deeply informs her work at UCLA. The Order of Deaconess and Home Missioner is a unique calling and status within The United Methodist Church as an order of laypeople committed to living vocational lives of love, justice, and service in relationship with The United Methodist Church. As a deaconess, Jeanne centers her vocational life at UCLA around sharing Christ with others in ways that "alleviate suffering, eradicate causes of injustice and all that robs life of dignity and worth, facilitate the development of full human potential, and share in building global community through the church universal."[11] As a lay professional, Deaconess Jeanne Roe Smith has led campus ministries in various contexts for the past twenty years. Deeply passionate about the role of the laity in the church at all levels, she frames her ministry with students in the larger calling of the office of deaconess: "I do this work with a real sense of social justice, community, and capacity building. I'm especially interested in engaging laity and local churches to join into this work"[12]

While Jeanne is passionate about empowering laity and engaging the local church in student ministries, she offers a sober warning against assuming that local congregations can engage in this work without the appropriate training and a critical awareness of student needs. She argues that the trend to relocate campus ministries back in the local church often puts undue stress on local congregations that feel unequipped or ambivalent about serving students. She reflects on this phenomenon:

> Many times, annual conference leadership assumes that a local church can do campus ministry because they are located next to a college, but sadly this is often not the case. Too often, campus ministry in the local church is an afterthought, intended only to bring students to worship. In these cases, it's not ministry on campus with students and faculty, it's more of an evangelism

> to bring students to their church, which is not what I understand the spiritual life and development of college students to be.[13]

Fortunately, the congregation in which the Wesley Foundation is nested has a healthy posture and understanding of their role and relationship to campus ministry, allowing Deaconess Roe Smith the space and support she needs to continue expanding and growing the ministry of the 580 Café.[14]

Growing into the 580 Café: Meeting Student Needs

Although the legal name of the organization is "Wesley Foundation Serving UCLA," the student ministry at UCLA is most widely known as "The 580 Café" or simply "580." The 580 Café is located at St. Albans Episcopal Church, where Deaconess Roe Smith began renting space for the Wesley Foundation in 2009. Moving from a building where the ministry had rented space before her arrival, Jeanne felt strongly that the ministry needed to find a location close to campus and accessible by public transportation. St. Albans, an aging Episcopalian congregation located directly across the street from the main entrance to campus and on a major bus line, served as the ideal location, and it had ample space available to rent. From this new location, Deaconess Roe Smith began to engage with UCLA students, faculty, and staff to identify the student needs that could be met through the Wesley Foundation. Through a process of listening, Jeanne connected to a larger conversation around the increasing student need for food and housing assistance. Working with the Office of the Vice Chancellor of Student Affairs, 580 Café developed as a direct response to the request for the campus ministry to provide free food and support for vulnerable students. Based in the Wesleyan concept of offering Christ, the 580 Café offers CHRIST (Compassion, Hope, Relationship, Inspiration, Solidarity, and Truth) in real and tangible ways.

Birthed out of a desire to meet basic student needs in ways that are relational and nurturing, the 580 Café began by serving prepackaged meals to students out of the rented space in St. Alban's church. When it started, 580 served only five or six students a few times a week, but as students began to create trusting relationships with Jeanne and with other students at the ministry, the numbers of students participating in the ministry increased exponentially over the next few years. Continuing in conversation with students and student groups, Jeanne incorporates student feedback into the 580 Café as it continues to blossom into a consistent and generative source of support for students. Cultivating a space of physical and spiritual nourishment and growth, the 580 Café meets a real and pressing need in the lives of students and has become a partner with other ministries throughout the city, such as Students 4 Students,[15] a student-run organization that rents space in a local church building focused on providing housing for homeless students.

Telling the Story: Bridging Student Ministries and Local Congregations

The unique institutional location of the 580 Café provides a vibrant opportunity for laity in a variety of local congregations to donate their resources to support UCLA students. The key for garnering ministry support for the 580 Café is providing the opportunity for congregations to hear and respond to its story. Deaconess Jeanne Roe Smith seeks to share the story of the 580 Café in a variety of ways, including attending Sunday worship services with students, publishing articles through denominational news outlets such as United Methodist Women and the General Board of Church and Society, as well as contributing to local news stories on the needs that students in California face.[16] Effectively sharing the story of the 580 Café with local congregations and community partners helps garner the additional resources the ministry needs to function, especially as the ministry continues to grow to meet the ever-increasing student needs. "As the students started engaging with us and telling us what they needed to study and thrive, we in turn started engaging United Methodist congregations, as well the host congregation [St. Albans] to figure out how we can provide more resources for the students."[17]

The historical relationship between the Wesley Foundation and United Methodist churches in Los Angeles has not always been strong; when Jeanne assumed the role of director in 2009, she addressed an expressed need to create or repair relationships with United Methodist congregations around UCLA. She did this primarily by attending worship at different churches each Sunday, offering to speak whenever possible to share the story of the Wesley Foundation and its emerging needs. Through this process, she discovered that many congregations, because of their preexisting relationships with alumni, students, and staff, did not feel the need to engage with the Wesley Foundation to serve students at the university.

Even so, Jeanne and students continued to share the story, emphasizing the need both for congregation-based student support as well as the unique ministry of the Wesley Foundation. "It is always important for me to emphasize to congregations that our presence at UCLA is not just for United Methodist students; this is a public university, and we are a progressive presence here for all students who might need us."[18] This process of intentionally sharing the story of the Wesley Foundation reinvigorated the relationship with several congregations in the area, inspiring local congregations to serve as vital partners as the Wesley Foundation began the process of becoming the 580 Café: "Sharing the narrative of our work helped to capture the imagination of some of our most primary partners; it helped the congregations to see that there is something that they can do to help."[19]

Encountering the stories of student need through Deaconess Jeanne Roe Smith's presentations, congregations began to see where their values overlapped with the Wesley Foundation, and new pathways for partnership emerged. For some congregations, the stories revealed a shared commitment to justice work around issues of immigration and LGBTQ inclusion in the church. For others, the stories of food insecurity and the lack of affordable housing opened a new congregational awareness:

> The food justice and housing issues surprised many congregations. Many [people] I spoke to had never considered that students at UCLA didn't have access to food. This reality is surprising, shameful, and embarrassing, and we should be doing something—not just as the church, but also as UCLA alumni in local congregations.[20]

In response to the intentional work of Deaconess Roe Smith, local congregations began to support the Wesley Foundation's growing student ministry through the 580 Café. Some congregations sent volunteers to help with operations, some sent financial donations, and others agreed to leverage their networks within the local community to increase awareness and help widen support for the ministry. Slowly, the network between local UMC congregations, the Wesley Foundation, and other community partners grew in strength, as did their relationships with the students they seek to serve.

Another layer of congregational engagement is the relationship between the 580 Café and the host congregation of St. Alban's Episcopal Church. Initially, the relationship between the Wesley Foundation and the congregation was simply a renter's agreement: The Wesley Foundation sought a physical location close to students and public transportation, and St. Alban's had space available to rent. As the ministry evolved into the 580 Café, the relationship between the congregation at St. Albans grew and changed. Whereas the initial permission to operate a food program for students relied heavily on rules that restricted how students were allowed to interact with the building and space, the relationship between the congregation and the students has a very different tone ten years later:

> It has taken seven years for the congregation at St. Alban's to embrace that the students are not coming to Sunday worship, but through their social justice committee we are developing relationships and doing work together, [and] they support us in a different way. They no longer try to get students to come and do things for them. The church now celebrates that the students are there daily, even though they don't often see them.[21]

Jeanne attributes this shift in the relationship between the 580 Café and the congregation to establishing quarterly neighborhood dinners where students and congregation members share a meal together in the church building. This simple act of breaking bread together has transformed the relationship between students and congregation members, teaching skills of dialogue across difference and allowing the congregation to encounter students and grow in relationship with them as beloved members of the body of Christ.

Oslo Central UMC—University of Oslo, Norway

Campus ministry does not exist in other countries in the same way as it does in the United States, but encountering the unique structures and challenges of other contexts has the power to expand our imaginations and inspire new ways of thinking about our own context. I've chosen to highlight the Norwegian United Methodist Church as it faces challenges similar to those faced by The United Methodist Church in the United States.

Institutional Location

The country of Norway has been affiliated with the Lutheran church, now known as the Church of Norway, since its independence from Rome in the mid-1530s. Norway cut official ties with the state church in 2017, ending a process begun by lawmakers in 2008 and creating a clear separation of church and state within the expression of their constitutional monarchy. Under the new separation of church and state, religious freedom is protected by the constitution, yet Lutheran values and affiliation remains the majority religious identification across the country.

Methodism arrived in Norway in the 1850s by way of a Norwegian sailor and missionary, Ole Peter Petersen, setting down roots first in the city of Sarpsborg and spreading quickly throughout working class neighborhoods in cities across the country. Historically, United Methodist congregations were founded in in the city centers of Norway and were deeply committed to engaging with the working poor. Although this is no longer exclusively true, this history continues to influence United Methodist identity and practice in Norway. United Methodism remains a small denomination, claiming only forty-six congregations and roughly 10,000 members as of 2014.

Oslo Center United Methodist Church is a 600-member congregation located in the city center. Founded in 1887, it is currently the largest United Methodist congregation in the city. The congregation does not have any formal relationship with the University of Oslo, which, like all universities in Norway, is public. Although there are state-funded chaplains from the Church of Norway at the university, they do not play the same role in cultivating spiritual life on campus as they might in the United States, and the congregation has no formal connection or relationship with the chaplains who serve at the university today.

Creating a Place for All People, Including Students

The congregational approach to student ministries at Oslo Central United Methodist Church is focused primarily on creating a vibrant intergenerational community. For this reason, most students involved at Oslo Central are not engaged through a specifically targeted student ministry. Marianne Munz, coordinator of children and youth ministries at Oslo Central UMC, reflects on the place university students hold in the congregation's ministries: "We have a general ministry for all people—everyone is welcomed always. This includes university students."[22] Oslo Central UMC seeks to cultivate intergenerational community as their first priority, reaching out to students not because of the uniqueness of their demographic but because of the support and identity offered in United Methodist community. In this way, the student identity is secondary to the United Methodist identity, as the congregation seeks to create space and community around denominationally held values and traditions.

> I want to emphasize the fact that our church is a minority church in Norway, a generally secular country, so doing student ministry is not something well

> known. However, we benefit from being a small church, because it gives us the possibilities of reaching out to all Methodists in person and establishing new relationships when they move to Oslo.[23]

In interviews, lay and clergy leaders at Oslo Central UMC all point to the significance of inhabiting a space of denominational minority within the larger culture. Distinct (and sometimes excluded) from the larger work of the Church of Norway and the Roman Catholic Church, which dominate the majority of Christian identity there, the United Methodist Church in Norway has used its Methodist identity as a means to gather and connect an intergenerational community around shared Wesleyan values and tradition. Although they value students in the larger life of their congregation, the primary focus of the congregation is on shared values, theology, and the connectional nature of The United Methodist Church. Reverend Maria Pedersen-Mong, pastor of Oslo Central UMC, emphasizes how important this intentional intergenerational approach can be to the way its congregation seeks to support students during the university time:

> Oslo is packed with student congregations, where everybody is in their twenties. We want our students to have a community where they can meet people [of] all ages, and that reflects all aspects of life. We think that by being a part of a congregation where you meet children, youth, and adults, both young and old, you get a family away from home.[24]

Focusing first on cultivating a vibrant intergenerational faith community, Oslo Central UMC seeks to serve students by being a place where people of all ages and backgrounds can find a home and a family.

Student+ and the Ebb and Flow of Student Ministries

Because of the intentional focus on cultivating a vibrant intergenerational community, the congregation at Oslo Central United Methodist Church does not always have a thriving student ministry; like many congregations close to universities, they experience seasons of active student ministry as well as seasons where there are few or no ministries specifically for university students. This ebb and flow of student engagement is a natural part of congregation-based student ministries, and it demonstrates the challenge of sustaining a consistent student ministry over time.

The last season of thriving student ministry at Oslo Central UMC began in 2011, led primarily by an active lay couple in the congregation, Audun and Irene Lohne Westad. Audun and Irene were inspired to create something specifically for students within the congregation, eventually creating a group called Student+, which began as a series of small-group gatherings for study, fellowship, and discussion aimed at connecting students and young adults more deeply to the life of the larger congregation. Led by Audun and Irene, Student+ grew over the course of several years. Audun attributes the group's success to its open environment and desire to help students make a deeper connection with others:

> I think the group was successful because there [were no prerequisites] to enter. The group was open for everyone, no matter if you were a direct descendent from John Wesley or just happened to attend something in the UMC for the first time. This was an easy way to get people to meet one another. Because most of the meetings were outside of the church building in private homes, we even found a way to reach out to those afraid to go to church.[25]

With focused personal invitations, accessible meeting environments, and cultivating relationships, Student+ held intentional space for students and other young adults at Oslo Central UMC. Even though Student+ operates in a network of relational small groups meeting in locations outside of the church building, an unintended consequence was bolstering student engagement in other areas of congregational life, including Sunday worship. Reverend Pedersen-Mong is clear that growing the Sunday service is not the goal of engaging with students, but it can be understood as one sign that students feel at home with the congregation: "I think we get an understanding of what we are doing right when the students continue to come, when they want to contribute, and when they tell us that they think our congregation is a warm, including place to be."[26]

Like many ministries focused on students, Student+ goes through seasons of lower participation. When asked why this thriving ministry sometimes dips into inactivity, Audun points to a variety of circumstances, such as the transience of student life and the availability of congregational leaders to organize and cultivate the necessary relationships for sustained student engagement. Reaching out to students at the large state-run university takes time and patience for congregation leaders. Audun was quick to point out, however, that even if the formalized structure of Student+ becomes inactive for a season, there are still activities offered for young adults through the church, and that some students are integrated into other areas of congregational life, such as teaching Sunday school. Ultimately, the ebb and flow of Student+ is held within Oslo Central UMC's larger emphasis on creating a warm and inviting intergenerational community, inviting students to participate in a United Methodist community of love, support, and service.

4

Regional Models of Student Ministry

There are many ways to serve students through the ministry of your local congregation that may not involve a direct relationship between your congregation and a college or university. Many regional programs exist throughout the United States that offer congregations ways to be in ministry with college students beyond their own local setting. These programs exist to serve specific student needs and often operate outside the timeframe of a traditional semester structure.

In the process of discerning God's call for your congregation, you may wish to consider the following alternative models of student support, either by identifying a regional network that already exists or by starting the process of creating one yourself. Finding regional partners to create something new may feel daunting, but it can begin with the communal discernment process outlined in chapter 5, using a slightly more expansive scope. Additionally, grants from organizations like the Lilly Endowment, the Forum for Theological Exploration (FTE), United Methodist general boards and agencies, or annual conferences may be available to help fund the creation of your new idea.

Community College Ministries (CCM)—Virginia, USA

Institutional Location

Community College Ministries (CCM) was founded in 1984 as an ecumenical Christian organization for the purpose of serving students at community colleges in the Commonwealth of Virginia. Responding to the ever-growing number of community colleges across the country,

CCM connects and empowers local congregations to serve the unique needs of community college students embedded in their communities. Recognizing that community college students are not served with the same resources and attention as those studying at four-year residential colleges, CCM seeks to meet this need in new ways by partnering both with local congregations and with the community colleges themselves. Currently, CCM exists as a network of United Methodist and Presbyterian Church (USA) churches in Virginia. Although ecumenical participation in CCM has evolved and changed over the past ten years, CCM remains a powerful example of the possibilities present anywhere community colleges exist.

The partnership between local congregations and community colleges is a natural and mutually beneficial relationship because of the significant overlap in mission and purpose. Reverend Steve Darr, director of CCM, identifies service to the greater community as a powerful common goal for both congregations and community colleges:

> Community colleges across the country understand service to the larger local community as their mandate. The mission of the community college is to support people who might not be in the mainstream of higher education and pursuing four-year degrees, but people who are outside the mainstream with specific vocational and career needs that community colleges are situated to meet.[1]

The institutional desire to serve the larger community, especially those who are marginalized by the mainstream, makes partnerships between community colleges and local congregations particularly compatible. Beginning in the early 1980s, the community college system in Virginia embraced a mandate to work together with similarly minded community institutions. This desire from the colleges inspired local congregations to create meaningful partnerships with local community colleges to work toward common areas of interest and concern within the local community.

Developing a Community College Ministry

The process of creating and establishing ministries through CCM involves an intentional process of information gathering. Once hired to direct the program, Rev. Darr and his team began interviewing stakeholders from across the state, including congregational leaders, community college administrators, college counselors, faculty, and students. Employing a network of ecumenical partners in the Catholic, Lutheran, Presbyterian, and Disciples of Christ traditions,

CCM gained critical input and feedback about the real and pressing student needs in their community. Through a continued process of listening, Rev. Darr and CCM seek to identify the most critical student needs in the state at any given time, then they work to create networks of local churches focused on addressing those needs. The result is the emergence of highly localized congregation-based programs that meet the needs of community college students in their community. The longevity of these highly localized programs varies: Some of the original programs have broken away from CCM as freestanding self-governing entities; some existed for a season and then stopped as student needs changed; and some continue to evolve to meet those changing student needs. Through a process of listening to stakeholders, leveraging networks, and adapting internally, CCM demonstrates the flexibility and attentiveness required to maintain a relevant student ministry over time.

One example of a program that emerged from CCM's work focuses its ministry around diversity and access to higher education. Responding to a national statistic that revealed white students accessed higher education at a fifty percent higher rate than students of color, CCM worked to create an ecumenical network of historically black churches in Roanoke, Virginia, to resource and empower young people of color to study at community colleges in their area. The program launched in 1986 as a partnership between two historically black mainline congregations and four community colleges. Meeting an urgent need in the community, the program quickly grew to serve the entire region through additional partnerships with area churches. As a result of these partnerships, by 1990 the enrollment of black students at the four community colleges increased 133 percent.[2] This dramatic increase was made possible through the creation of congregation-based neighborhood centers to support and resource the students. One such center, established by Danville Community College at Camp Grove Baptist Church in the city of Danville, continues to resource high school students today by offering access to college counselors, homework assistance, mentoring, computers, and the availability of programs specifically aimed at empowering students of color to achieve their college aspirations.

Ministry in the Margins

Students at community colleges often fall outside the age demographics of the traditional undergraduate students. Community college students tend to be older, already part of the workforce, caregivers for children, and represent a wider ethnic and racial diversity than is frequently present at four-year residential institutions. Because community college students are already living and working within the local community, many churches assume that students who desire to be part of a congregation are already connected; however, this often is not the case. Reverend Darr urges congregations not to overlook the opportunity to reach this student demographic:

> The vast majority of community college students are local, and yet because the community college population represents a hugely diverse sector of society and a slightly older population—the reality of that is that all of those in the community college system, they may have had a church connection somewhere, but their needs are far greater than were getting met by remote congregations that are not addressing the critical needs that they have in the community colleges. Those of us working in the community college realize that there are huge areas of outreach and mission potential for community college students because of the gaps that exist in student services.[3]

One of the most powerful reasons to consider creating a ministry tailored for community college students is the shared mission to meet the needs of those underserved in your local community. Reverend Darr reflects on the great potential and opportunity present for congregations to partner with local community colleges: "One of the great things about community colleges is that everyone on campus is looking for an ally. They are looking for partners to make their work and outreach in the community successful. There is a general eagerness to work with churches as well as community-service agencies and schools. It's very open." Despite the mutually held mission to serve the greater community, many churches do not engage in meaningful ministry with community college students. Reverend Darr attributes the absence of community college ministries in local churches to a lack of congregational awareness about the potential for ministry with these students:

> I think many churches have never thought about community college students as an emphasis of ministry. Many churches don't think about it because they see community colleges as embedded within their community, and for the most part, those colleges don't have students coming in to live in residence—leaving their home and church to move into their community. They don't have the influx of students [whom] churches see as [being in] vulnerable times in [their] lives, so it's often not a top concern.[4]

Community college students often face significant socioeconomic challenges, yet their needs are often less visible to congregations because frequently they are already local residents and can easily fade into the background.

Despite the general lack of awareness, Rev. Darr is hopeful about the capacity for local congregations to respond to the needs of community college students: "In my experience, when you talk to churches about what the needs are of students in the local community college, they are wholly enthusiastic about supporting ministry with that population."[5] Effectively communicating the areas of need is key to CCM's success in inspiring congregations to serve community college students. Once congregations understand that the needs of community college students align with their church's mission, congregations often feel compelled to help. For example, one of CCM's current areas of focus is providing support for the large number of community college students who have come out of Virginia's foster care system, as discussed below. Often, these students are still healing from childhood trauma and lack the family and social support that exist for other students. Raising awareness about the unique needs of this student demographic gives local churches an opportunity to provide missing support that may be necessary for the completion of a degree or certification.

Ministry with community college students, especially those with marginalized identities, often takes a very different form than ministry with traditionally aged students at four-year institutions. Somewhat less whimsical than midnight pancake parties and free pizza on the quad, supporting the needs of community college students may look like providing access to counseling or financial support for rent, utilities, food, or childcare: "There are many community college students who are living in poverty. For example, if a student can't afford their utility bills or [can't afford] to feed their kids and also pay their tuition bill, churches are in an ideal position to help."[6] Although providing this kind of support for students is often not what congregations envision when beginning a student ministry, it is a deeply influential type of ministry in the lives of the nontraditional students it serves.

For congregations to embrace this kind of student ministry, they need to be willing to encounter the stories of the students who are in need of this kind of support. In Rev. Darr's experience, when CCM is able to educate congregations around the pressing needs of community college students, congregations become increasingly receptive and embrace the opportunity to serve as a mission and outreach ministry. Because of his experience with local churches in Virginia, he believes in the power of increasing congregational awareness: "If churches know where the needs are and how to meet them, they are eager to support these students."[7]

Creating and Cultivating Strategic Partnerships

The network created by CCM allows congregations to engage with local community college students through grassroots programs and partnerships around specific and contextually relevant student needs. The way congregations address these needs depends on the cultivation of strategic partnerships with other local congregations and organizations. For CCM, the process of creating partnerships and empowering grassroots programs and services is ongoing. CCM is always looking for new ways to partner with others around specific areas of need. Reverend Darr emphasizes this as a foundational element of successful community college ministry: "It is practically impossible to do this work alone; in every program we do, the first thing we do is to look for allies and partners to meet our goals in ministry."[8] Local congregations eager to meet student needs are ideal partners in ministry.

In 2018, CCM applied this process toward the goal of addressing the needs of community college students who have experienced the foster care system as children. Estimating that more than 5,000 students studying in Virginia fit into this category, CCM began the process of communicating the need and cultivating strategic partnerships in local communities all over the state to empower others to support these students.

> For young people in their twenties who have come out of foster care, 54 percent are unemployed, 31 percent are homeless, 80 percent of the young women in that group have become pregnant since leaving foster care, and 32 percent of those young women before they are eighteen-years-old. Of this population, 60 percent of young men in this group have been convicted of a crime; many have spent time in jail; and there is only a 3 percent success rate in educational opportunities after high school. There is a huge challenge to the young people and their transition into economically and socially productive life after foster care.[9]

Rev. Darr believes that local congregations, partnered with other community organizations, are in a unique position to help support students in this demographic as they seek to heal and flourish as adults. To facilitate the kind of partnering required to provide such support in local communities, CCM is joining a larger initiative called "Open Table."

Open Table relies on teams in churches and other community organizations to support individual students who have come out of foster care. CCM's partnership with Open Table emerged as Rev. Steve Darr sought out agencies and organizations within the state that held overlapping concerns, missions, and values.

> When I started hearing the concern about students coming out of foster care from my interviews with community college counselors, I reached out to agencies I was already in relationship with through United Methodist and Presbyterian churches. I eventually had a meeting with United Methodist Family Services in Richmond, Virginia, to talk to them about whether there were areas in their programming within their family services that might include foster students within their large network in the state of Virginia. I was looking for places where their mission and ours would overlap and [where] we could work together.[10]

Rev. Darr had similar conversations with other organizations, such as the Presbyterian Children's Home Association, administrators from local community colleges, and representatives from the Open Table organization, with the hope of leveraging networks to collaborate. From these meetings, there emerged a network of people across the state committed to raising awareness and empowering local congregations, as well as other community organizations, to create support teams in communities across the state for students coming out of the foster care system. Although this program is still in the launching stage, it is a powerful example of what can happen when people and organizations connect to identify and articulate common missions and values and establish networks of support that serve the real needs of students.[11]

Calling 21, Virginia Annual Conference of The United Methodist Church

Institutional Location and History

Calling 21 is a strong example of a successful and adaptive regional program that allows local congregations to connect with and support students from all over the state of Virginia.[12] With visionary leadership and an adaptive structure, the Calling 21 program allows local congregations to host undergraduate student interns each summer. Interested students apply through the Virginia Annual Conference of The United Methodist Church and are matched with compatible host congregations by the Calling 21 design team. Accepted students receive training and orientation at Shenandoah University at the beginning of the summer. For the duration of the internship, the students stay with host families arranged through their host congregations and receive support and mentoring from clergy, lay leaders, and intern support teams. Representatives from hosting congregations receive comparable training each year, coordinated through the Office of Clergy Excellence located in the Virginia Annual Conference office. Student interns engage in leadership opportunities in their host congregations tailored to their gifts and to their calling in ministry. This program offers many opportunities for congregation members to interact with the students, whether through serving as host families, joining the intern support team, serving as mentors, or simply creating informal relationships through mutual service each summer.

Since its birth in 1996, Calling 21 has served ninety students through its network of more than forty-three United Methodist churches. Calling 21 exists as a partnership between Shenandoah University, the Virginia Annual Conference, and a design team embedded in the conference's Office of Clergy Excellence that serves as a governing board. Of the ninety student alumni of the program, thirty-eight have gone on to seminary after college, thirty-three of whom have chosen the path toward ordination or licensed ministry in The United Methodist Church. Seeded with a grant from the Fund for Theological Exploration, Calling 21 was created to name, notice, and nurture college students in the mid-Atlantic region discerning a call into ministry. Addressing the need to reinvigorate a culture of call within the region, Calling 21 cultivates leadership skills, vocational discernment, and intergenerational affirmation within the context of the local church.

Current design team chair and former student intern Rev. Meghan Roth Clayton describes the current mission and vision of the program:

> At the foundation, Calling 21 is an opportunity for college-age students to see with new eyes what work they may be called to do and be about. If that is ordained ministry, that's wonderful, and we'll celebrate and help them along that path, but we also want folks to know that this is an opportunity to discern other vocational paths. If we can help provide those kinds of lens[es] and [highlight] what students do in the world as meaningful and impactful, we've achieved our goals and mission with the program.[13]

Seeking to meet the need for vocational discernment and exploration in an intergenerational context, Calling 21 provides a compelling alternative way for congregations to meaningfully support a college student each year.

Creating a Network of Support for Students

One of the most influential aspects of Calling 21 is the network of support it creates for its student interns. Offered as a short-term summer experience, Calling 21 provides an opportunity for students to create meaningful intergenerational relationships with laity and clergy outside their immediate context. This expands the students' network of support and can help sustain their vocational discernment and aspirations well past graduation. Even though Calling 21 is designed as a short-term, relatively low-risk, summertime experience, the deep intergenerational relationships cultivated between student interns and congregation members increase the impact of the program over the long term. Reverend Roth Clayton reflects on this aspect of the program:

> I would say that although Calling 21 is a short-term commitment, it becomes an extended experience because of the ways [in which] students can build relationships and support. If it is a positive experience for students and congregations, Calling 21 can become an extended transformational experience for all involved.[14]

The role of mentoring and intergenerational relationships is an essential component of Calling 21's success. A powerful testimony to the impact of the program's mentoring and the relational network is the current chair of the Calling 21 design team. Reverend Meghan Roth Clayton's journey with Calling 21 began when she was a student at the College of William & Mary in Williamsburg, Virginia. Part of the first Calling 21 intern cohort, Rev. Roth Clayton served as an intern at St. Luke's United Methodist Church in Yorktown. The relationships Rev. Roth Clayton made with laity and clergy through her participation in Calling 21 influenced her vocational trajectory toward seminary and ordination in The United Methodist Church: "I absolutely believe in the impact significant [Calling 21] mentors put in place for me, the network of support they provided as people who care deeply about young people."[15] Reverend Roth Clayton is not alone in her experience of Calling 21. Many alumni of the program share similar stories of how the intergenerational relationships built during their internships guided their vocational journeys during and after college.

A Congregational Perspective: St. Luke's United Methodist Church, Yorktown, Virginia

St. Luke's United Methodist Church in Yorktown is one of the longest-standing congregational partners for Calling 21. It has hosted student interns each year since the program began in 2006. The idea that St. Luke's UMC could support students in this unique way was initially brought to the congregation's leadership by their district superintendent. The decision to host an intern was then affirmed by St. Luke's pastoral and congregational leadership through a process of intentional discernment. Excited about the prospect of serving students in a new way, St. Luke's stepped out in faith, and participation in Calling 21 has now become a vital part of their congregational identity.

The Revs. Doug and Clara Gestwick, who served as the senior and associate pastors of St. Luke's between 1996 and 2017, can attest to the impact Calling 21 has had on the congregation. Leaning into the notion of noticing, naming, and nurturing young people, Rev. Doug Gestwick saw Calling 21 as an opportunity to help young people discern their vocational path, but he also saw it as a way to shape congregational identity:

> No matter what vocation you have in life, oftentimes if you get to the bottom of it, a teacher is a teacher because someone along the way said, "You know, I think you'd be gifted at teaching"; an engineer is an engineer because someone said the same. The church forgot for a generation to say to young people, "Hey, you really show signs and gifts for ministry. Have you ever thought of going into ministry?" . . . I saw Calling 21 as an opportunity for our congregation to see itself as a calling congregation.[16]

In part, St. Luke's chose to continue participating in the program as a host church in order to awaken the congregation to its larger identity as one that notices, names, and nurtures the call of those in its midst. Reverend Gestwick credits St. Luke's engagement with the Calling 21 program as a force that has shaped the congregation's identity. Reverend Gestwick reflects: "I wanted the congregation to ask itself how we cultivate a culture of call not just with the eight weeks we have a student in the summer, but how do we self-identify as a calling congregation?

What does that mean for us to do that? Over time, that vision played out in beautiful ways at St. Luke, and I think Calling 21 was a big part of that."[17]

While the Calling 21 program is designed with student identity and faith formation at the center of its mission, St. Luke's UMC demonstrates that intentional and prolonged engagement with this program has a positive effect on congregational identity and call. It is important to note, however, that the benefits the congregation experienced through the program were a byproduct of their service, not the goal. Although engagement with Calling 21 student interns over the years resulted in hiring younger church staff and engaging differently with the young-adult demographic in the church, the congregation's focus was always on serving and affirming the student intern.

Adaptive Structure: Redefining Vocational Discernment

Providing space for students to engage in intentional vocational discernment is an essential part of the Calling 21 program. Originally, this process focused on discerning a call into ordained ministry. Reverend Meghan Roth Clayton reflects on the ways Calling 21 offered space for her own discernment:

> There was thorough self-discovery; there were tools provided for personal discernment, personal spiritual formation; there was ample opportunity provided for me and the other interns to serve and try on things for size. I think this is an important thing for young people, to be able to experiment: Try on preaching, try on serving in a local outreach capacity. It gives students a low-risk environment [in which] to put different hats on, to see what feels right and what doesn't.[18]

Similarly, Rev. Carl Chapman, part of the 2009 cohort of student interns, identifies the impact of his experience as an intern in Sterling, Virginia. "Sterling UMC was really helpful for me as I explored my call. Through interactions with staff and with a support team that they put together for me, I was able to review what had been going on in my life, and I was able to discern whether a call to ministry was for me."[19] Carl is one of many Calling 21 alumni who currently serve as clergy in The United Methodist Church.

When reflecting on the impact of Calling 21, it is important to notice the ways in which the program has changed over the years to continue to meet the needs of the students it serves.

Originally birthed out of a desire to identify, encourage, and empower college students to consider ordained ministry in The United Methodist Church, the Calling 21 design team, in partnership with the Virginia Annual Conference and Shenandoah University, are continually asking questions about how the program might shift to meet emerging student needs.

One current shift within Calling 21 is the way the program approaches vocational discernment. While there remains a hope that the program will help those students who are called toward ordained ministry, there is an increasing focus on a broader definition of a call into ministry. Instead of solely focusing on ordained ministry as the pinnacle of vocational discernment, Calling 21 now seeks to equip students for wider vocational discernment through the lens of their faith. Through mentoring and practical experiences, students are encouraged to consider the ways God is calling them to serve through their particular passions and training. This expanded lens allows students to understand any professional calling as a form of ministry, regardless of where that call takes them. Students who are discerning a call to any number of fields, such as nursing, physical therapy, teaching, athletic training, and many other areas, can understand their work as ministry as they seek to participate faithfully as members of Christ's body and citizens of the kingdom of God.

5

Discerning from the Inside Out

Developing Internal and External Processes

Internal Process: Congregational Discernment

Now we have arrived at the difficult part: honestly assessing the internal work required of your congregation to effectively do the work you are called to do and cultivating the external relationships necessary to actually do the work. If your goal in student ministry is to have a gaggle of college students sitting in your pews on Sunday morning, you will want to reassess this goal before you begin. Starting a student ministry will likely not drastically change the number of students who show up to worship on Sunday morning. It's just not going to happen, and if it does, it won't happen because you set student worship attendance as your goal. Luring students into your building to fulfill congregational nostalgia, to pad your statistical tables with the coveted "young adult" demographic, or to have people to set up tables for your annual chicken barbeque are not good reasons to start a student ministry. Those are self-serving goals, not student-serving goals. The kinds of intergenerational support available for students in local congregations can be invaluable for their holistic identity and faith formation, but the potential and beauty of that congregational support is often sabotaged by misguided and unexamined assumptions, expectations, and measures of success. If you'll only be happy if your congregation gets a good "return" on its investment in students, you should likely reassess whether you are actually called to this work. This may sound harsh, but it is the truth. Too many well-meaning congregations unwittingly fall into a consumerist trap when it comes to student ministry, as if students are only worth your time, energy, and money if they have something desirable to offer you. The kingdom of God does not work this way. Our congregations should not either.

Self-awareness is the first step in any good process of discernment, and your desire to seek greater self-awareness through asking difficult questions is your first step on the journey. If you are going to build an effective student ministry based in your congregation, you will need to commit to these, and many more, soul-searching questions as you discern how God is calling you forward. Every congregation has a different culture, history, and process of communal discernment. This section seeks to honor the uniqueness of your own congregation, while offering a process through which you can engage in the work of discernment with honesty, vulnerability, and transparency. The process below breaks down five distinct and vital elements necessary for communal discernment around God's call to serve students in your context. This section is meant to be not a cookie-cutter program for success but a guide for intentional discernment as you prepare your congregation to serve students with clear (and realistic) expectations and flexibility.

Step 1: Assemble Your Team

You likely arrived at the idea of starting, building, or rebuilding a student ministry because someone in your congregation is passionate about serving students. Passion is the lifeblood of ministry, and building a good team has the potential to put feet on your dreams. Your first step in creating a student ministry is to capture that passion and combine it with other like-minded stakeholders in your congregation. You can do this by strategically creating a team of people to serve as the core and catalyst for this ministry. This step is especially crucial during the initial discernment and building stages. The size, scope, and structure of your team will depend on the size and culture of your congregation, but here are some general guidelines and tips.

Who Assembles the Team: Even when led by laity, clergy support can be critical to the success of any new ministry in a congregation. This means that open and transparent conversation with your pastoral staff about your excitement and intention to build a discernment team for student ministries is essential from the start. For this reason, it is wise to schedule a meeting with your pastoral leadership as a part of the team-assembling process in order to gain permission and support and to receive additional suggestions for others who would be good to include on your team.

Who Is Around the Table: The primary task when assembling your team is to ensure you have a passionate and diverse group of people who are each committed to the task at hand. Because of the scope and nature of pastoral relationships, your pastoral leadership may have additional insights into the gifts and passions of people who are on the margins of your congregations yet might be a good fit for the team. Thoughtfully consider whether there are individuals within your current church leadership who would be essential to the success of your proposal, but resist the urge to include only those who already hold significant positions of leadership. If there are gatekeepers in your congregation around certain ministry areas, such as finance or trustees, be sure to include people on your team who can help gain access to the hearts and minds of these important stakeholders. Your pastor can be an important resource in thinking thoughtfully about who might be best in this regard.

Team Size: Your team size will vary, based on your congregation's size and interest in the project. Because your student-ministry launch team is primarily tasked with facilitating congregational discernment and garnering larger congregational support, it is important that your team be small enough to be flexible and discerning, yet large enough to generate a diversity of perspectives. A small, intentionally diverse team of five to eight people is ideal for this work. More than eight people will make scheduling difficult, while fewer than five will limit the capacity for collaboration and imagination within the group. If you cannot find five passionate people in your congregation to help discern God's call and nurture your vision for a student ministry, it may be difficult for you to gain the larger congregational support needed to launch a successful student ministry.

Scope and Structure: The effectiveness and success of any team depends on clearly communicating the commitments and expectations of its members. Before you begin asking people to be a member of the team, establish a clear mission, expectations, and a timeframe. This will help those whom you ask to be on your team make a realistic and informed commitment. Here are some examples:

> *Mission:* This team will discern God's call to create a student ministry based in our congregation. This team will create a proposal for the first step of this ministry and present it to the church's administrative council at the June meeting.
>
> *Expectations:* Team members are expected to attend monthly two-hour team meetings between September and the end of May, attend one community

> partner interview, and respond in a timely manner to calls, e-mails, and text messages.
>
> *Timeframe:* This team will commit to nine months of work (September–May) and will reassess the scope, composition, and timeframe of the team at the end of May.

In addition to communicating clear and concrete expectations and the scope of the team's work, it is vital to establish a team leader (or coleaders) to organize and facilitate the team's work. Even if your congregation prefers a flat team structure, your team will be most effective if one person is responsible for caring for the administrative and organizational tasks of the team, such as creating an agenda, sending e-mails and texts, and ensuring that the team operates within the mutually agreed-upon guidelines and boundaries. The more organized, transparent, and intentional your team culture, the more discerning and effective its work. You honor the members of your team and the call God has placed on the life of your congregation when you respect one another by creating and maintaining healthy boundaries and practices.

Step 2: Intentional Discernment: Pray and Study Together

Once you have a committed group of passionate team members, your work of intentional discernment begins! Setting aside time for prayer and Bible study is an essential step in your discernment process. If you are following these steps as a guide, steps 2 and 3 as outlined here will likely be interconnected and mutually informing as you engage deeply with the movement and the Spirit through scripture study and as you apply the wisdom you glean to the particularity of your call and context.

The way your team approaches prayer and study will vary, depending on the culture of your congregation, as well as the timeframe established by your team. Ideally, your team will set aside at least half of its designated meeting times for structured prayer and Bible study. The content of your Bible study will depend on the particularity of your call and the needs of your congregation, but be cautious not to choose scripture that will only reinforce what you already think you know about your call. Consult together with the team, and come to a consensus about the content of your scripture study, giving thoughtful attention to the larger narrative arc of your congregation's scriptural engagement through recent sermon series, established Bible studies and small groups, or congregation-wide initiatives; it is likely that God's call to create a student ministry is tied to the larger movement of God in the life of your congregation!

In addition to budgeting intentional time for prayer and Bible study with your launch team, you may want to consider finding creative ways to integrate any particularly helpful scriptural reflections that emerge from your team into the larger life of the congregation. This can be done in consultation with your pastor and other congregational leaders in a variety of ways, including brief scripture readings and reflections at the beginning of committee meetings (such as administrative council, finance committee, or trustees), integrating similar scriptural content into existing small-group structures, or incorporating similar scriptures or themes into times of corporate worship.

To set your team up for success, clearly determine and agree to the time commitment and expectation for prayer and study. For example, the team could devote several weeks or months to meeting together for the sole purpose of praying and studying. Another approach might be to set aside the first half of every meeting to pray, read and discuss a scriptural passage, or assign a scripture passage for team members to read and contemplate between each meeting, making the commitment to discuss the passage at the beginning of every meeting. There are any number of ways to set aside time and energy for this task, but allotting adequate time for communal prayer and study is an essential component of both discerning the specifics of God's call for your community as well as building the necessary theological foundation for your work. Do not let your anxiety or impatience tempt you to skip this aspect of the process. If you skip ahead to the practical aspects of your ministry plan without giving space for your team to root your project in scripture and theological engagement, you will lose a valuable opportunity to frame—and reframe—the particularity of God's call for your congregation, in this time and place, with the timeless challenge of the gospel message.

Step 3: Identify and Articulate God's Call, Theologically Framed

Once you've done the intentional work of sitting with God in prayer and studying scripture in community, your team is ready to identify and articulate God's call on your congregation as it relates to your student ministry. You should be able to write this down in a few clear sentences. This call should be informed by how you encountered the movement of God in scripture. For example, after a period studying the parable of the sower, your team might articulate God's call in this way: "In the parable of the sower found in the synoptic Gospels, we encounter an image of God sowing seeds with abandon. In this parable, we hear God's call for Audubon Park United Methodist Church to sow seeds of extravagant love in the lives of students on the campus of Gonzaga University, without concern for reciprocation." Even if your understanding of how God is calling you to live out your call may change, framing your desire to create a student ministry with a theological value derived from scripture will enable you to remain rooted and also effectively communicate your vision and call to other stakeholders in your congregation.

Although your team will likely explore several different scripture texts as a part of your times of prayer and study, seek to identify the text or texts that most resonate with the group as your foundational scripture for this ministry. This text will serve as the foundation and theological frame for beginning your student ministry. Helpful questions to guide this work might include: *What does this scripture say about who God is? What does this scripture say about who God is calling our congregation to be? How does this scripture inform how God is calling us to treat other people? How might this scripture inform how we as a congregation serve students?*

Step 4: Craft a Ministry Abstract

Now that your team has a theologically rooted articulation of how and why you feel God is calling your congregation to serve students, it is time to flesh out the practical details of your first steps in creating or expanding your student ministry. We will call this document a "ministry abstract." Your ministry abstract will help your team communicate your vision and needs to others in your congregation in order to gain resources and support for your ministry. Your team can use your ministry abstract as you seek to gain critical support from individuals and committees within your congregation, such as the pastoral staff (although hopefully your pastor is already involved in this project at this point!), administrative council, finance committee, or board of trustees. Depending on the scope of your project, you will likely need each of these groups to support your proposal, especially if you seek to use your congregation's financial, building, or other property resources to support your ministry. As you craft your proposal, you may want to begin with a general document that outlines the overarching vision, theological support, and resources needed for the project. After this document is finished, you can tailor the proposal to the specific individual or group to which you are appealing for specific resources, just as you would with your résumé or cover letter when applying for a job. Your proposal should include the following sections: a theologically framed vision, a description of what the ministry will be (and maybe the first step of what that might be), goals and measures of success for the ministry, potential ministry partners, and resources needed to support the ministry. These documents will help you create clarity regarding what and how you are trying to communicate about your vision for student ministry and what support you need from your congregation to be successful in your endeavor.

Example Ministry Abstract That Accommodates a Large Vision Not Yet Fully Clarified

Vision: To create a student ministry at University United Methodist Church to support students on the campus of Generic College through direct partnership with the United Methodist Ecumenical Chaplaincy in the Office of Spiritual Life.

Theological Support: In the parable of the sower, we encounter an image of God sowing seeds with abandon. In this parable, we hear God's call for our congregation to sow seeds of extravagant love in the lives of others without concern for reciprocation. Although we have a historical and proximal relationship with Generic College, we do not currently support the United Methodist Ecumenical Chaplaincy in the way we feel God calls us to do. We believe that God is calling us to reestablish our support for students through the chaplaincy, even if it will not "yield" increased numbers in our worship attendance or congregational programming in our building.

Ministry: We do not yet know what form our ministry with students at Generic College will take, but we hope to work closely with the United Methodist Ecumenical Chaplain to determine what her greatest needs might be at this time. Our team has generated several ideas, including supporting a weekly free meal for students on campus, opening up designated space in our church building for Generic College students to use as needed, and creating a "foster family program" where members of our congregation "adopt" a college student for a semester as a means to build relationships and support for students.

Goals and Measures for Success: Our team feels God is calling us to sow seeds of love in the lives of students on the campus of Generic College without expectation of reciprocation. For this reason, our primary goal is to extend signs of love into the lives of students. We strongly feel that we should frame our goal in terms of relationships built and nurtured. Our goal is for our congregation to create meaningful relationships with at least five students before the end of the academic year, assessing our progress by collecting stories from congregation members and students in the spring.

Potential Partners: The primary partner needed to live into our call to serve students at Generic College is the United Methodist Ecumenical Chaplain in the Office of Spiritual Life.

Resources and Support

- *Prayer:* We need the congregation of UUMC to be in intentional prayer for our students as well as our willingness to respond to God's call to serve them.
- *Financial*: $2,000 annually to support ministry programming with students on campus; $1,000 in this fiscal year to create a student lounge in the church building; $500 annually to stock the lounge with snacks and other resources.
- *Property:* Permission from the trustees to renovate space in the church building to be used as a student lounge.

Example Ministry Abstract That Accommodates a Specific Vision

Vision: To create a student ministry at University United Methodist Church to support students on the campus of Generic College through direct partnership with the United Methodist Ecumenical Chaplaincy in the Office of Spiritual Life.

Theological Support: In the parable of the sower, we encounter an image of God sowing seeds with abandon. In this parable, we hear God's call to for our congregation to sow seeds of extravagant love in the lives of others without concern for reciprocation. Although we have a historical and proximal relationship with Generic College, we do not currently support the United Methodist Ecumenical Chaplaincy in the way we feel God calls us to do. We believe that God is calling us to reestablish our support for students through the chaplaincy, even if it will not "yield" increased numbers in our worship attendance or congregational programming in our building.

Ministry: After consulting with the United Methodist Ecumenical Chaplain in the Office of Spiritual Life, there is a need to support students on campus who are struggling with food insecurity. We feel God is calling us to support this ministry by donating healthy food options to the campus food pantry and supporting the chaplaincy's monthly free meal held on campus.

Goals and Measures for Success: Our goal is to provide five shopping bags of healthy food to the campus food pantry and $200 toward a free meal for students each month for this academic year.

Potential Partners: The primary partner needed to live into our call to serve students at Generic College is the United Methodist Ecumenical Chaplain in the Office of Spiritual Life.

Resources and Support

- *Prayer:* We need the congregation of UUMC to be in intentional prayer for our students as well as our willingness to respond to God's call to serve them.
- *Financial*: $1,800 from the missions budget to support a free meal on campus ($200 per month, September–May)
- *Donations:* We will depend on donations of food items from the congregation each month to meet our goal of five shopping bags of food each month donated to the food pantry.

Step 5: Put Feet on Your Dreams

Once your ministry abstract is complete, celebrate! It is important to mark this important milestone in your journey of discernment. This document will serve as the foundation of your work moving forward. It will likely grow and change as you begin to widen the circle of support for your vision from the wider congregation and, eventually, from external partners such as chaplains, Wesley Foundation directors, or university staff and faculty. Now that your initial ministry abstract is complete, you can make a plan for how you will communicate it more widely and integrate the feedback you receive. Your team now has the opportunity to share your passion and vision for this ministry with others.

How you decide to engage with your wider congregation to gain support for your project will depend on your congregational culture. With the wisdom of the people on your team, discuss what the best approach might be. In some churches, it may be best to appeal first to the governing committee or board, such as the administrative or church council (or its equivalent), and then connect with committees like the trustees or finance if you have specific requests for monetary or property support. It may be the case that in your congregation, a different approach will be more fruitful—for example, perhaps working with your pastor to introduce your proposal to small groups or in a congregational meeting, with an open time for feedback. Whatever your approach, it will be important that your team creates a mechanism for people in the wider congregation to offer feedback in the form of both affirmation and suggestions for adaptation. People invest in that which they create; offering an opportunity for the wider congregation to give input into your proposal will create a greater likelihood that they will support the endeavor in other ways.

While your team is working on your internal communication strategy within the congregation, you should simultaneously identify and implement a strategy for communicating with and gaining support from any external partners who are necessary to your work. These partners, identified in your ministry abstract, will depend on the college or university structure in your context. At a private university, these external partners might be a chaplain, spiritual-life dean or director, campus minister, or director of a service-learning office on campus. At a public university or community college, these external partners might be college staff or faculty, career counselors, or other support staff. Depending on the circumstance, your external support partners might be other nonprofits in the area that have overlapping goals and values as the ministry you are seeking to create (for example: addressing food insecurity, homelessness, or sexual violence). Creating and nurturing external relationships will strengthen your endeavor and likely will create unexpected and fruitful partnerships. Similar to the need to create space for feedback from your congregation, finding ways to ask for feedback from potential external partners will also help you find people who are interested and invested in supporting your work.

External Process: Institutional Bridging and Student Engagement

It may be tempting to try to create and sustain a student ministry all on your own. Resist the temptation. No person is an island, and although it may seem appealing to create a student ministry that you can claim all for yourself (and your congregation's statistical tables), creating trusting relationships with institutional partners, and even with other congregations, will greatly impact the effectiveness of your work. These relationships can be complicated for a variety of reasons but are essential to the success of your fledgling ministry. Relationships are essential to every aspect of ministry, and this is no exception.

Institutional bridging is not rocket science; it is relationship building. You simply need to figure out who has the power to give you access to students or resources that you need and begin to form a relationship with those people. Before you begin to reach out, take an inventory of the connections that already exist in your congregation. Do you have staff or faculty members from the college? Do you have alums or (even better) trustees? Are there any other connections that might help your congregation be seen by the university as credible or trustworthy? Is there a way to leverage those networks? While you consider what connections you already have, do a little research on the institution itself: What kind of university is this institution? Do they have a campus ministry or office of spiritual life? Is there a Wesley Foundation or other organization that supports Protestant students on campus? From whom do you need permission to put up flyers, promote at tables, or host events on campus? The answers to these questions will help you focus your energies and limit the number of e-mails, texts, or phone calls you will have to make.

From here, the process is simple: Once you know whom you need to communicate with, send an e-mail or make a phone call. Make it short, friendly, and invitational: "Hi! My name is Colleen Hallagan Preuninger. I am the pastor of UUMC down the street. Our congregation feels called to increase our support for the students on your campus. Would you be free for a phone conversation in the next few weeks to talk a little bit more about this?" Don't worry about being formal or fancy; speak like a human and try to make a connection. If that person does not return your message, e-mail or call again with a request to set up a short meeting to talk about possible ways your congregation might be able to support students on their campus.

The reality is that many colleges and universities are wary of outside Christian congregations or leaders whom they do not know, and not without reason. Much harm has been done to students because of Christian leaders and congregations that do not have student needs at the center of their motivations. Bear this in mind as you seek to make connections. Do not be easily offended or discouraged if it takes time to build trusting relationships with university staff and administrators or even with campus ministers and Wesley Foundation directors. If God is calling you to this, and if your motivations are rooted in this call, God will make a way, even if it takes a while. Be patient, be kind, be vigilant.

The final and most important group of people with whom you will need to communicate are students. This may initially be difficult if you do not have any students connected to your congregation when you begin this process; but to have an effective student ministry, you *must* find a way to consistently listen and respond to student needs in your specific context. The importance of this cannot be overstated. Without a way to gain and respond to student feedback, your ministry will not be a student ministry, and your ministry will fail. Student voices are essential to any student ministry. To create an effective student ministry, you must actively seek out and prioritize student voices and respond to student needs by adapting your ministry.

CONCLUSION

Next Steps and a Future Filled with Hope

Everything is changing, all the time. This is especially true in the lives of students as they navigate their university years. As the church, we have a powerful opportunity to journey with students through the rapids of their college education by coming beside them as a means of support, encouragement, and challenge as the intergenerational body of Christ. We, as communities of Christ followers, have the power to help meet their needs—physiological, relational, and spiritual—if we are willing to put in the intentional work of discernment, self-awareness, and placing student needs above congregational fears or expectations. As with any relationship, it takes work to become self-aware and responsive to the needs of people that are different from your own. Students' needs are not the same from generation to generation, context to context; truly serving students means providing consistent opportunity to listen to their real and expressed needs, and to respond in a way that prioritizes student needs over congregational expectations. This is difficult and life-giving work; the road will not be easy, but if you choose to travel, it will be filled with hope.

In the previous five chapters, I have demonstrated that creating a vibrant student ministry is deeply contextual and requires both congregational awareness and flexibility to adapt to the constantly shifting needs of students in the higher-education context. I have lifted up examples of effective congregation-based student ministries at both public and private universities, as well as regionally based models. My hope is that these examples are presented in such a way that you can see both the successes and the challenges of each context and that you might be encouraged and inspired to try something new.

Throughout this book, I have argued that with intentional congregational discernment, theological rooting, and intentional planning that prioritizes student voices, your congregation has the capacity to build a student ministry that supports and nurtures students in a critical time in their faith and identity formation. I have emphasized congregational process and discernment over the particularity of programmatic structure or content. I have done this because I believe that creating a theologically engaged and self-aware foundation for student ministry in your congregation is essential if you seek to create a relevant student ministry that has the capacity to adapt enough to be sustainable over time.

The church often seeks to plug ministry holes with programmatic fixes; these kinds of quick fixes might work for a season, but they will not be sustainable over time. It is better to do the hard work of internal discernment and external relational bridging up front, slowly shifting your congregational culture to be increasingly the warm, inviting, relational intergenerational community it is meant to be. Once you have prioritized a theologically framed posture toward building your student ministry that places student voices at the center, you can easily access the wealth of resources available to inform the content of your ministry (for small groups, leading mission or service learning trips, creating food or shelter resources, and so on). I have included a few at the end of this book that may help you in this work.

The landscapes of our lives and institutions are changing. As the author of Ecclesiastes reminds us, the reality of change is not new, but it can feel disorienting nonetheless. As traditional sources of campus ministry funding decrease, the ways in which spiritual and religious life take place on campus are changing: College and universities are decreasing staff in their offices of spiritual life and expanding the responsibilities of the staff who remain; annual conferences are investing less money in higher education; and general boards and agencies are decreasing their capacity to support students through scholarships and other resources. In some ways, this shift in the landscape of student support feels like a death; and in many ways, it *is* a death. We can name this reality and mourn, just as the disciples mourned the reality of Jesus' death at the foot of the cross on Good Friday.

At the same time, as Christians, we are Easter people. We are the women proclaiming the tomb empty; we are the disciples called to speak in a multiplicity of languages on Pentecost. We are the church, birthed by the Spirit of God. In the face of this death, we, as the church, are called to be the hands and feet of the resurrected Christ. In this case, this means that your congregation is called to be Christ's presence and support to students who are increasingly underserved. In light of the Resurrection, we have nothing to fear. In light of Pentecost, we are empowered to speak and serve in ways that are yet unimagined and seemingly impossible. In light of all this, your congregation has the capacity and power to meet this emerging and urgent need in the lives of students. The only question that remains is, will you answer the call?

FOR FURTHER READING

Online Resources

Collegiate Ministry Resources through the General Board of Higher Education and Ministry (GBHEM): www.gbhem.org

Discipleship Ministries, Resources for Young People: www.umcyoungpeople.org

Forum for Theological Exploration (FTE): www.fteleaders.org

General Board of Church and Society: www.umcjustice.org

The Neighboring Movement: www.neighboringmovement.org

Potential Sources for Grants and Student Scholarships

Forum for Theological Exploration (FTE): www.fteleaders.org

General Board of Higher Education and Ministry (GBHEM): www.gbhem.org

The Lilly Endowment Inc: www.lillyendowment.org

Cultural Competencies and Intersectional Theology

M. Shawn Copeland, *Enfleshing Freedom: Body, Race, and Being* (Minneapolis, MN: Fortress Press, 2010).

James H. Cone, *The Cross and the Lynching Tree* (Maryknoll, NY: Orbis Books, 2013).

Yvette A. Flunder, *Where the Edge Gathers: Building a Community of Radical Inclusion* (Cleveland, OH: Pilgrim Press, 2005).

Patrick B. Reyes, *Nobody Cries When We Die: God, Community, and Surviving to Adulthood* (St. Louis, MO: Chalice Press, 2016).

Andrew Root. *Faith Formation in a Secular Age: Responding to the Church's Obsession with Youthfulness* (Grand Rapids, MI: Baker Academic, 2017).

Generational Scholarship

Mark E. Hanshaw and Timothy S. Moore, General Editors, *Intersections: Faith, Church, and the Academy* (Nashville, TN: GBHEM, 2018).

Kara Powell, Jake Mulder, and Brad Griffin, *Growing Young: Six Essential Strategies to Help Young People Discover and Love Your Church* (Grand Rapids, MI: Baker Books, 2016).

Corey Seemiller and Meghan Grace, *Generation Z Leads: A Guide for Developing the Leadership Capacity of Generation Z Students* (CreateSpace, 2017).

James Emery White, *Meet Generation Z: Understanding and Reaching the New Post-Christian World* (Grand Rapids, MI: Baker Books, 2017).

Curriculum and Resources for Use with College Students

Sarah E. Bollinger and Angela R. Olsen, *The Awakened Life: An 8-Week Guide to Student Well-Being* (Nashville, TN: General Board of Higher Education and Ministry, 2019).

David E. MacDonald, *Benedict on Campus: Eight Spiritual Disciplines for Collegiate Ministry* (Nashville, TN: General Board of Higher Education and Ministry, 2018).

NOTES

Chapter 1

1. "Community College Facts at a Glance," US Department of Education, Digest of Education Statistics, 2001, Table 244, https://www2.ed.gov/about/offices/list/ovae/pi/cclo/ccfacts.html.
2. For more information about Wesley Foundations or to find another validated United Methodist College Ministry in your local context see https://www.gbhem.org/education/collegiate-ministry.
3. For more information on Newman Centers, http://www.newmanconnection.com.
4. For more information about Cru, https://www.cru.org.
5. For more information about legal challenges to Intervarsity's leadership policies, https://intervarsity.org/about-us/press-room/campus-access-issues/legal-challenges.
6. For more information about BASIC, https://basiccm.org.
7. For more information about FCA, http://teamfca.org.
8. For more information about Young Life, https://www.younglife.org/Pages/default.aspx.
9. "Religion Among the Millennials," Pew Research Center Religion and Public Life, February 2010, https://www.pewforum.org/2010/02/17/religion-among-the-millennials.
10. For further reading, see *A Family Genogram Workbook* by Israel Galindo, Elaine Boomer, and Don Reagan, (Galindo, 2017); *Extraordinary Relationships* by Roberta Gilbert (Leading Systems Press, 2017).
11. James 2:14-16 NRSV
12. For more information on hunger and homelessness at UCLA, see "Homelessness on Campus," CBS News Sunday Morning (January 20, 2019), https://www.cbsnews.com/news/homelessness-on-campus-the-toughest-test-faced-by-tens-of-thousands-of-college-students-in-america; and Kimberly Yavorski, "The College Students Who Are Starving in Silence," Pacific Standard (July 6, 2017), https://psmag.com/education/college-students-starving-in-silence.
13. Chase Sakett, Dr. Sara Goldrick-Rab, Katherine Broton, *Addressing Housing Insecurity and Living Costs in Higher Education: A Guidebook for Colleges and Universities* (U.S. Department

of Housing and Urban Development, 2016), https://www.huduser.gov/portal/publications/HousingInsecurityInHigherEd.html.

Chapter 2

1. "History of National UMC," National United Methodist Church, https://nationalchurch.org/history.
2. American University, About, https://www.american.edu/about/history.cfm.
3. Interview with Rev. Joey Heath-Mason, October 9, 2018.
4. Heath-Mason interview.
5. Heath-Mason interview.
6. Campus Kitchens, Get Started, https://www.mightycause.com/organization/The-Campus-Kitchens-Project.
7. Interview with Patrick Landau, October 25, 2018.
8. Interview with Patrick Landau.
9. "About: Our Mission," Grace United Methodist Church, http://gracewinfield.com/about-2.
10. Southwestern College, "History," https://www.sckans.edu/connecting-to-sc/history.
11. Interview with Rev. Lora Andrews, August 30, 2019.
12. Interview with Lora Andrews.
13. Interview with Rev. Ben Hanne, December 3, 2018.
14. Interview with Ben Hanne.
15. Interview with Ben Hanne.
16. Interview with Ben Hanne.
17. Interview with Rev. Lora Andrews, August 30, 2019.
18. Interview with Lora Andrews.
19. Interview with Lora Andrews.
20. Interview with Rev. Ben Hanne, December 3, 2018.
21. For more information about Audubon Park UMC, see http://audubonparkumc.org/welcome.
22. For more information about Whitworth University, see https://www.whitworth.edu/cms.
23. For more information about Gonzaga University, see https://www.gonzaga.edu.
24. Interview with Rev. Geoff Helton, January 1, 2019.
25. Interview with Geoff Helton.
26. Interview with Geoff Helton.
27. Interview with Geoff Helton.
28. Interview with Geoff Helton.
29. Interview with Geoff Helton.
30. Interview with Geoff Helton.

31. Interview with Geoff Helton.

Chapter 3

1. Interview with Megan Otto, September 19, 2018.
2. Interview with Megan Otto.
3. Interview with Megan Otto.
4. Interview with Megan Otto.
5. Sarah E. Bollinger and Angela R. Olsen. *The Awakened Life: An 8 Week Guide to Student Well-Being* (Nashville, TN: GBHEM, 2019).
6. Interview with Rev. Bill Frisbie, January 15, 2019.
7. Interview with Bill Frisbie.
8. Interview with Megan Otto, September 19, 2018.
9. Interview with Megan Otto.
10. Interview with Megan Otto.
11. For more information about the office of deaconess and home missioner, see https://www.unitedmethodistwomen.org/dhm.
12. Interview with Deaconess Jeanne Roe Smith, January 25, 2019.
13. Interview with Jeanne Roe Smith.
14. For more information about the 580 Café, see www.580cafe.com.
15. For more information about Students 4 Students, see https://www.s4sla.org/home.
16. For further reading on hunger and homeless at UCLA, see "A Spiritual Home at UCLA," Response Magazine (June 2014), https://www.unitedmethodistwomen.org/news/a-spiritual-home-at-ucla. Also see "Free Cafe Helps Struggling UCLA Students Eat," NBC Los Angeles, November 8, 2011, https://www.nbclosangeles.com/news/local/UCLA-Free-Meals-133495093.html; and Amber Feezor, "Ministry with: 580 Café," Church and Society, The United Methodist Church, April 16, 2018, https://www.umcjustice.org/news-and-stories/ministry-with-580-cafe-658.
17. Interview with Deaconess Jeanne Roe Smith, January 25, 2019.
18. Interview with Jeanne Roe Smith.
19. Interview with Jeanne Roe Smith.
20. Interview with Jeanne Roe Smith.
21. Interview with Jeanne Roe Smith.
22. Interview with Marianne Munz, February 8, 2019.
23. Interview with Marianne Munz.
24. Interview with Rev. Maria Pedersen-Mong, February 7, 2019.
25. Interview with Audun Westad, January 19, 2019.
26. Interview with Rev. Maria Pedersen-Mong, February 7, 2019.

Chapter 4

1. Interview with Rev. Steve Darr, October 15, 2018.
2. Interview with Steve Darr.
3. Interview with Steve Darr.
4. Interview with Steve Darr.
5. Interview with Steve Darr.
6. Interview with Steve Darr.
7. Interview with Steve Darr.
8. Interview with Steve Darr.
9. Interview with Steve Darr.
10. Interview with Steve Darr.
11. For more information about the Open Table Movement in Virginia or how your congregation might get involved in your local context, visit https://www.theopentable.org.
12. For more information about Calling 21, see https://vaumc.org/Calling21.
13. Interview with Rev. Meghan Roth Clayton, January 16, 2019.
14. Interview with Meghan Roth Clayton.
15. Interview with Meghan Roth Clayton.
16. Interview with Rev. Doug Gestwick, December 13, 2018.
17. Interview with Doug Gestwick.
18. Interview with Rev. Meghan Roth Clayton, January 16, 2019.
19. Interview with Rev. Carl Chapman, December 20, 2018.

Printed in the USA
CPSIA information can be obtained
at www.ICGtesting.com
JSHW060002120324
58905JS00002B/8

9 780881 779356